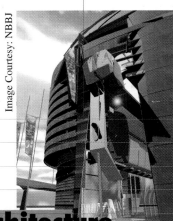

Image Courtesy: NBBJ

Digital Architecture
Digital Architecture

M. Saleh Uddin

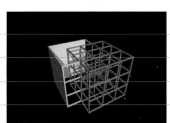

Digital Architecture

McGraw-Hill

New York San Francisco Washington, D.C. Auckland Bogotá
Caracas Lisbon London Madrid Mexico City Milan
Montreal New Delhi San Juan Singapore
Sydney Tokyo Toronto

Library of Congress Catalog-in-Publication Data

Uddin, M. Saleh, 1955-
Digital Architecture
ISBN 0-02-065814-5

McGraw-Hill

*A Division of The **McGraw-Hill** Companies*

2 3 4 5 6 7 8 9 0 CA 9 0 4 3 2 1 0
ISBN 0-07-065814-5

The sponsoring editorfor this book was Wendy Lochner, the edting supervisor was Penny Linskey, and the production supervisor was Pamela Pelton.

Printed and bound by Color Art

McGraw-Hill books are available at special quantity discounts to use as premiums and sales promotion, or for use in corporate training programs. For more information, please write to the Director of Special Sales, McGraw-Hill, I 1 West 19th Street, New York, NY 1001 1. Or contact your local bookstore.

This book is printed on recycled, acid-free paper containing a minimum of 50 percent de-inked fibre.

Design, electronic layout and composition by M. Saleh Uddin (author).

Front cover digital drawing: Graha Kunigan Office Tower, Jakarta, Indonesia, by Ellerbe Becket.
Back cover digital drawing: Vertical Park for the URA Singapore by Ken Yeang of Hamzah & Yeang.

Digital Architecture

CONTENTS

Advanced Media Design (for Kohn Pedersen Fox, Robert A. M. Stern Architects) • Anthony Ames Architect • Natalye Appel Architects • Architecture Research Office • Arquitectonica • R.L. Binder, FAIA • Centerbrook Architects • Einhorn Yaffee Prescott • Office dA • Davis Carter Scott • Deiss and Associates with Oliver + Ray Architects • Delphi Productions • Peter Edgeley • Ellerbe Becket • Felderman + Keatinge Associates • Form:uLA • Fox & Fowle Architects • Carl Hampson • HDR Architecture • HLW International • HNTB • House + House Architects • Inglese Architecture • Murphy/Jahn (Helmut Jahn) • The Jerde Partnership International • Kajima Corporation • Kiss + Cathcart Architects • KovertHawkins Architects • John Lumsden • Machado and Silvetti Associates • Morphosis • Eric Owen Moss Architects • NBBJ • Nelson Design • Cesar Pelli & Associates • Pentagram Architecture • Perkins & Will • Polshek and Partners Architects • Richard Rauh & Associates • Resolution: 4 Architecture • Rogers Marvel Architects • Schwartz Architects • TRO/The Ritchie Organization • Tsao & McKown Architects • Bernard Tschumi Architects • van Dijk Pace Westlake Architects • Venturi, Scott Brown and Associates • Vistaara Architects • Voorsanger & Associates Architetcs • Wendy Evans Joseph Architects • Ken Yeang

Acknowledgements
Acknowledgements

I would like to extend my appreciation to all the architects and designers who generously participated in this project and took their time to explain their drawings via e-mail, fax, phone, and overnight mail. I especially thank them for their prompt response to my many requests, queries and for maintaining deadlines.

I thank Bryan Cantley of Cal Poly Fullerton, Richard Rauh of Richard Rauh & Associates, Lisa Tilder of Ohio State University, and Andrej Zarzycki of TRO for taking extra effort to construct or rewrite text for specific explanations on short notice.

Peter Pran and Joey Myers of NBBJ, Steven House of House + House, A. Scott Howe of University of Oregon, John Maze of John Design Collaborative, Deepika Ross of Perkins & Will, deserve special thanks for their enthusiasm and trust in this project.

Special acknowledgement to my editor Wendy Lochner of McGraw-Hill for her endorsement and support to the original proposal of the book.

My special gratitude is extended to Paul Davis who not only overwhelmed me with submissions for the beginning section, but also helped me with graphic suggestions. Although I never met him in person, we spent almost an entire day communicating back and forth with text and image revisions through e-mail and telephone.

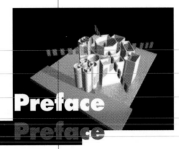

Preface

Preface

The primary intent of the book is to highlight the role of digital media in overall design and professional practice of architecture. To achieve that goal, this publication features more than 50 selected architects' and designers' cutting-edge design ideas represented through computer graphics, specifically three-dimensional modeling.

The beginning section of the book deals with the various types of uses of computer media by designers subdivided into Conceptual Studies, Dimensional Orthographics, 3D Modeling and Rendering, Desktop Publishing Formats, Digital Analysis, Digital Hybrids, and Digital Multimedia. Each subdivision in this section shows use of such kinds of computer presentation with examples.

The main section of the book catalogs alphabetically selected architects and their current design projects presented through three-dimensional digital media with accompanying text. Profile of the office or designer, use of digital media, drawing process and image technique, hardware and software used and design concept constitutes the explanatory text for each designer's work.

It is the author's hope that this book will be a source of ideas for current trends in digital media for architectural design presentation as well as a good reference material for initiating new design ideas.

Mohammed Saleh Uddin
Baton Rouge, Louisiana

1

Introduction

Image: Eric Owen Moss Architects

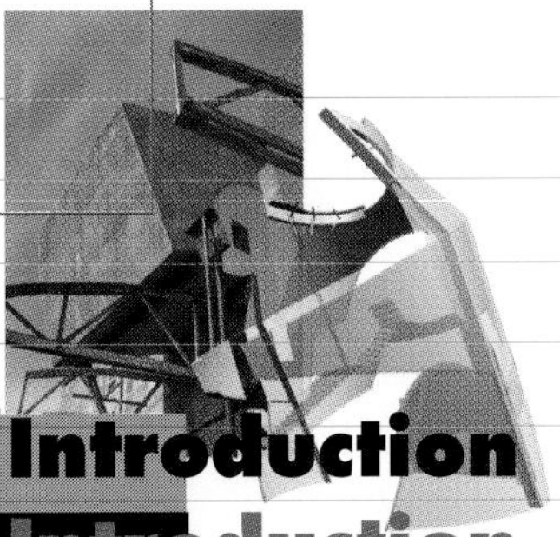

Introduction

Introduction

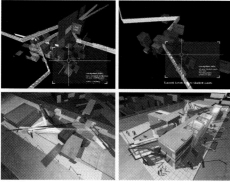

Matthe Baran's conceptual schematic design for a School of Architecture.

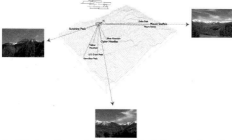

Architecture Research Office's analysis between long distance and near views for the Sunshine Messa House.

Zareen Rahman's study of three-dimensional 'sight-lines' in progressive luminosity for an urban project.

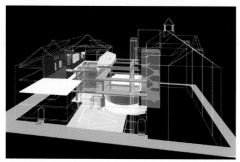

Rogers Marvel Architects' schematic 3D model for reconstruction of Pratt Institute School of architecture.

INTRODUCTION

There is no debate whether the computer technology is a positive or negative influence in the design process of architecture. That was an issue when AutoCAD was the only mode of adaptation of computers in architecture. Although technological changes have arrived within the architectural profession at a slower pace than other fields, recent use of 3D modeling and multimedia applications portrays significant changes that are occurring currently in architectural visualization and representation.

Practitioners in 1980's have blamed architecture schools for not preparing new graduates for the new technology, especially CAD. That trend has changed during 1990's. Now fresh graduates bring more diverse and comprehensive computer knowledge than ever before. On the other hand the universities have always focused on total learning of computer environment, not just autocad. Most curricula now emphasize 2D drawing, 3D modeling, desktop, and multimedia and their various use in conceptualization, as well as representation of design ideas. Between 1992 and 1996 a significant number of schools adopted Form•Z, a new 3D modeling and rendering application designed initially for architects, with the big question that the practicing offices at that time were not using Form•Z. Today that question does not exist since most offices create their models with Form•Z.

By surveying all the projects featured in this book it is clear that architects and designers are settling down on their choice of software. Although not intended to be a complete list, it can be summarized that the following application programs have become widely accepted for architectural use at present time. For production drawing AutoCAD, for modeling and rendering 3D Studio, and Form•Z (some use of Microstation, MiniCAD, ArchiCAD is noticeable), for page layout QuarkXpress and PageMaker. For image manipulation Adobe Photoshop remains the invariable choice. Adobe Premiere, PowerPoint, and Director have common use for multimedia authoring and presentation.

Architects and designers have begun to experiment very recently with the digital media that reaches beyond the purpose of mere presentation. The use of various modes include: conceptualization, design synthesis, design presentation (2D drawing and 3D modeling and rendering), desktop publishing (brochures and reports), animation (movies, and videos), web-page authoring, multimedia and hypermedia authoring (slide show, interactive presentation, QuickTime VR movies). It should be noted that the drawings in this book were drawn (in most cases) before the construction of a building, or in few cases for unrealized buildings. Such drawings often play an important role in the development of architectural ideas and new movements, and may be different from drawings that only document a building. Drawings in this segment of the book illustrate examples that are non-conventional in nature and explore the digital media beyond typical representation.

Matthew Baran's conceptual schematic design for a School of Architecture was developed simultaneously as a digital preseence in the internet and a model for the built environment. The program spaces were represented by various cubic nodes, which would dock in a logical relation to one another.

The images by *Architecture Research Office* for the Sunshine Messa House in Colorado take advantage of computer modeling to analyze the context of the vast site and the designed building. The relationship between long distance and near views specific to each room of the house was studied in 3D model environment to adjust window and mullion sizes and their appropriate location.

Zareen Rahman's study of three-dimensional 'sight-lines' in a site plan represents a series of vertical layers of "force plane" rendered in progressive luminosity and translucency that intends to produce a lucid and cogent spatial analysis for an urban project. Through the mode of translucency hidden patterns could emerge and be read in parallel with the existing site fabric.

Rogers Marvel Architects' 3D model for reconstruction of Pratt Institute School of Architecture combines abstraction and color rendering in a schematic manner to emphasize certain aspects of renovation work.

Conceptual recording of random reality and imagination in 3D computer model by *Morphosis* represents embroynic grammer of form.

Eric Owen Moss's digitally stitched photo montage for Pittard Sullivan Office Building unfolds a space that is impossible to document or record in conventional photograph.

Richard Jensen's site and floor plans illustrate digital integration of technical line drawing and pictorial image of colorful landscape. The integration takes into account combining raster and vector imaging.

The image for Oklahoma Civic Center Music Hall by *Polshek and Partners* illustrates a powerful exploded cut-away perspective emphasizing constituent components and floor plan footprint.

Conceptual embroynic grammer of form by Morphosis.

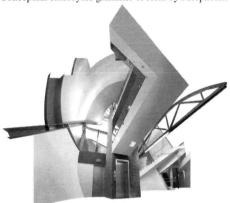

Digitally stitched photo montage by Eric Owen Moss.

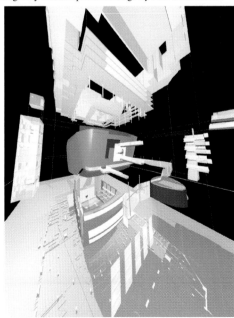

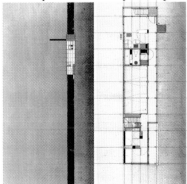

Integration of technical line drawing and pictorial image by Richard Jensen.

Exploded cut-away perspective by Polshek and Partners for Oklahoma Civic Center Music Hall.

Kiss + Cathcart's complex curving shape comprised of over 1200 glass and photovoltaic modules for the Hamburg's Electrical Utility.

"Fabrications" construction at the Museum of Modern Art, by Office dA employs digital computation and laser cutting.

NBBJ's use of 3D electronic data to build 3D physical models.

Kiss + Cathcart's complex curving shape comprised of over 1200 glass and photovoltaic modules most of which are different sizes and shapes for the Hamburg's Electrical Utility takes advantage of computer modeling and rendering for appropriate simulation.

On the other hand ecology is the primary concern for *Ken Yeang.* The project for Continuous Vertical Park and Expo 2005 Tower by *Ken Yeang* explores and brings together ecological concerns and bioclimatic approach to the design of tall buildings.

For *Office dA,* the digital media has permitted its designers an unquestionable fluidity between the process of conceiving, drawing, and manufacturing that was virtually unprecedented. For the "Fabrications" project at the Museum of Modern Art, *Office dA* has constructed a folded plate structure using a technology that had never been attempted at that scale or level of complexity with digital computation and laser cutting.

Exploration with 3D technology at *NBBJ* is not just limited to 3D electronic data. For design studies, design team(s) extract 3D electronic data from the computer and use this data on various manufacturing tools to build 3D physical models that are more tactile and can physically relate the objects' scale. Whether it is laser cutting Plexiglas and wood or the use of SLA (Stereo-Lithography) polymer resins to create a physical model, the design team(s) now have an increasing palette and resourceful tool combinations. Consequently, the two design methods (virtual and physical) complement and inform each other throughout the design process.

These examples as well as works featured by more than 50 selected architects and designers in this book speak to the power of the digital media that is too important to be ignored.

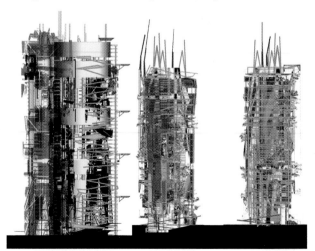

Ken Yeang explores and brings together ecological concerns and bioclimatic approach to the design of tall buildings.

2

Selected Terminologies
in Digital
Representation Media

Selected Terminologies
in Digital Representation Media

SELECTED TERMINOLOGIES IN DIGITAL REPRESENTATION

3D: Three-dimensional. Having, or appearing to have length, width and depth.

AIFF: an acronym for Audio Interchange File Format. A standard for exchanging sound information between applications.

Algorithm: A list of specific steps or a set of rules leading to the solution of a problem.

Alpha Channel: In a 32-bit image, 8-bits are used for storing the red color information, 8 are used for the green information and 8 are used for the blue color information. The remaining 8-bits can be used by some applications to store masking information for compositing images together. A common use is to layer a graphic over a background or an animation over a live video. The alpha channel is used to store the anti-aliasing (see below) information so that the composite is seamless.

Ambient Light: A type of light that illuminates all the surfaces equally and which is always present. Its intensity and color are user defined parameters. Ambient light does not cast shadows, but fills in the shadowed areas of a scene.

Analog Computer: A computer that processes data input in a continuous form or data represented as an unbroken flow of information.

Animate: To give motion to an object or a group of objects over time.

Animation: A series of images (called frames) that create an illusion of movement when displayed rapidly in sequence.

Anti-aliasing: A method of smoothing jagged edges that appear in computer generated images when pixels of contrasting colors occur next to each other.

Applications Program: Software written to solve a specific problem.

Architecture: The design and organization of the components of a computer system. The structure of a database.

ASCII (American Standard Code for Information Interchange): A standard system that can represent 128 different characters.

Bezier: A type of spline curve (see spline).

Bit: The smallest unit of information that can be held in memory.

Bitmap: An image composed of pixels of specified colors. A bitmap can be any resolution with any number of colors. The most common bitmap formats are PICT and TIFF.

Boolean Operation: They are the 'Union', 'Intersection', 'Difference', and 'Split' operations, which can be applied to solids, closed 2D modeling shapes lying on the same plane, and closed drafting elements.

BPI (Bits Per Inch): A measure of capacity, or density, of storage media.

BPS (Bits Per Second): A measure of line capacity or data transmission speed.

B-splines: A type of spline curve whose control parameters include knots. It can be generated in any degree.

Bug: A logical or clerical error.

Bump Map: A grayscale image used to give a surface the illusion of ridges or bumps.

Byte: A group of adjacent bits that form a character.

C: A computer language particularly suited to writing operating systems and special programming applications.

Cache Memory: Cache memory refers to memory chips located on the system board. Data that someone accesses often is stored temporarily in cache memory. Cache memory saves processing time because the computer can simply reach into cache memory for data storage instead of normal memory, which takes longer.

CAD (Computer-Aided Design): The use of computers to

prepare and test dimensional drawings for engineering, architecture and mechanical fields.

CAM (Computer-Aided Manufacturing): The application of computers to accomplish manufacturing tasks.

Chip: A solid-state device (Integrated Circuit) containing a complex group of transistors and electronic circuits etched on a small piece of silicon, about 1/16 inch square.

Clock (System Clock): A component of the control unit of the central processing unit that sends out pulses that regulate the opening and closing of electronic circuits within the CPU.

COBOL (Common Business-Oriented Language): A programming language used in business.

Computer: An electronic device capable of receiving input, processing data and generating output according to stored instructions, with high speed and accuracy.

Controlled Curve (c-curve): A curved line generated from a vector line (polyline), which functions as a control line. When stored, c-curves carry their controls and can be subsequently edited and changed.

Controlled Objects (c-objects): Objects that are stored with the control parameters used for their generation. Such objects can subsequently be edited and changed, while they remain c-objects.

CPU (Central Processing Unit): The portion of the computer that performs calculations, controls its operation, and contains primary memory.

Cursor: An icon displayed on the screen at the position of the mouse. Cursor icons vary, depending on the active preferences and the operation being executed.

Defaults: The values assigned by the system at start up to parameters that affect the execution of operations, as well as other settings of the system.

Desktop Publishing: The application of computers to the preparation of typeset documents with graphics such as newsletters and reports.

Digitizer: An input device that converts pictures, lines or drawings into x-y coordinates.

Disk: A metal or plastic plate coated with ferromagnetic material on which data may be recorded.

Diskette: A thin flexible plastic disk coated with ferromagnetic material on which data may be recorded. Also referred as flexible disk, floppy disk.

DOS (Disk Operating System): An operating system that stores the bulk of its instructions on magnetic disk.

Dot Matrix Printer: An impact printout device that forms characters by striking the ends of a group of wires or rods arranged in a pattern.

E-mail (Electronic Mail): Message sent by the transmission of electronic pulses rather than by the transfer of physical documents.

EPROM (Erasable Programmable Read Only Memory): A solid state storage device capable of read only memory that can be removed from the computer and exposed to ultraviolet light in order to be reprogrammed.

Extrusion: The creation of a three-dimensional object by pushing out a two-dimensional outline to give it height, like a cookie-cutter.

Fiber Optics: A cable consists of bundles of glass or plastic fibers that are able to transmit data in the form of light.

File: A collection of related records treated as a unit.

Flat Shading: A fast rendering algorithm that gives each facet of an object a single color. It yields a solid representation of objects without taking a long time to render.

Font: A set of characters molded on a printing element.

FORTRAN (FORmula TRANslating system): A programming language that resembles mathematical notation and is used primarily for scientific applications.

Fractal: A mathematically generated pattern that is endlessly complex. Fractal patterns often resemble natural phenomena in the way they repeat elements with slight variations each time.

Gouraud Shading: A rendering algorithm that provides more detail because it averages color information from adjacent faces to create colors. It is more realistic than flat shading, but less realistic than Phong shading or ray tracing.

007

GUI: Graphics User Interface

Hard Copy: Output in a permanent physical form, such as a paper printout, that can be read or viewed by people.

Hardware: The physical component or equipment used to input, process, and output data.

Helix: An object or revolution derived by revolving a source shape about an axis, while the source shape is also displaced in a direction parallel to the axis of revolution. Helixes can be wire objects, surfaces, surface solids, or solid objects.

Hidden Line: A modeling plotting method by which only the visible edges of the objects are displayed. Edges on the back sides of objects or edges that are hidden by other objects are not shown.

Image Mapping:A two-dimensional image (in the form of a PICT file) applied to the surface of an object. It is a method of wrapping a picture around an object. Image mapping is convenient for placing pictures or text onto objects, for example, a label on a model of a bottle.

Impact Printer: An output device that forms characters by striking a raised letter against a ribbon, imprinting the characters on a sheet.

Ink Jet Printer: An output device that forms characters from a continuous stream of ink droplets.

Interactive Program: A computer program that permits data to be entered or the course of programming flow to be changed during its execution.

K: An abbreviation for the prefix "kilo," meaning 1,000 in decimal notation. In computer terminology, an abbreviation for a value equal to 1,024.

Keyframe: A frame in a sequence which specifies all of the attributes of an object. The object can then be changed in any way and a second keyframe defined

Kilobyte (KB): 1,024 bytes.

Knurl: A pattern consisting of a grid of pyramidal shapes extending from a surface.

LAN (Local Area Network): A communications system that links workstations within a geographically limited area,

usually by coaxial cable, to enable users to share computer resources.

LCD (Liquid Crystal Display): A visual display in which output images are formed by a liquid suspended in an electronic field.

Lathe: A lathe object is created by rotating a two-dimensional shape around a central axis. It is convenient for creating 3D objects like glasses, vases, and bowls.

Loft: Loft (also called skinning) stretches a surface over a series of two-dimensional "ribs" or cross-sections. The surface will have the shape of each cross-section at the cross-section, and will blend smoothly from one to the next.

Map: a) To project an image onto the surface of an object. b) Images and effects that are applied to a surface to affect its appearance in a certain way (e.g. marble map, wave map, etc.)

MB (Megabyte): About 1million bytes, or 1,024 Kbytes

Menu: A list of options and choices of programs available or processing modules within a program from which users select.

Mesh: A pattern of cells superimposed on a surface or a complete object. A mesh pattern typically consists of rectangular cells, but it can also be a triangular pattern.

Meshed Terrain Model: A terrain model whose land form depicting surface is a rectangular mesh of adjustable density, whose points are positioned relative to the elevations of the contour lines from which the terrain model is developed (see terrain model).

MICR (Magnetic Ink Character Recognition): Recognition of characters printed with ink that contains particles of magnetic material.

Microcomputer: A miniature computer manufactured on a small chip, using solid-state integrated circuitry, that possesses characteristics of a large system.

Model: Something composed of one or more objects. Models often resemble something in the real world. A "guitar model" might contain separate objects for the neck, head and the body.

Modeling: Creating and arranging objects, placing lights and cameras, and applying surfaces to objects.

Modem: Modem stands for MOdulator-DEModulator. The main function is to convert the digital signals from a computer into the analog signals suitable for transmission along phone lines. As phone lines eventually become entirely digital, modems will disappear. Also called a coupler.

Morphing: An abbreviation for "metamorphosing". The changing of one shape to another, usually performed during an animation.

Motherboard: The motherboard is the main circuit board to which cling the CPU, the ROM chips, all expansion boards, and the computer's memory chips.

Motion Path: The interpolated path generated by animation software from keyframes which define an object's position and orientation in space at different time intervals.

Mouse: An input device that is moved about on a tabletop and directs a pointer on a screen.

MS-DOS: Microsoft Disk Operating System. There are also other versions of Disk Operating Systems.

Multiprocessing: A system in which two or more central processing units are wired together to share processing task.

Network: A system of computers and terminals interconnected by communications circuits.

Noise: A mathematically defined pattern that uses variable degrees of randomness to generate its color pattern.

NTSC: Video signals standard in the United States and Western Hemisphere.

OCR (Optical Character Recognition): The ability of certain light-sensitive machines to recognize printed letters, numbers, and special characters.

Orthographic View: A view in which an object's distance from the viewer has no effect on the size at which it is drawn. Plan, elevation, and section views are orthographic in nature.

Pan: Moving the image displayed on the screen in any direction determined by mouse input. It resembles window scrolling, except that the latter is restricted to horizontal and vertical moves only.

Parallel Port: A parallel port is a socket to connect a parallel device (like a printer) to a computer.

Perspective View: In a perspective view, the farther an object is from the viewer, the smaller it appears.

Phong Shading: A rendering algorithm that creates high-quality surfaces. Phong shading calculates a color for every pixel on an object's surface. The path that the light follows is not calculated in Phong Shading (as it is in ray tracing) so advanced lighting effects like reflection and transparency can not be represented.

Photorealism: A quality in an image that makes it look as though it was created by photography. Originally a technique in painting.

PICS File: A single Macintosh file consisting of a series of PICT images.

PICT File: A standard format used by many Macintosh graphics programs.

Pixel: A single dot of light on the computer screen; the smallest unit of a computer graphics. Short for "picture element".

Point Light: A light source that emanates from a single point in space in all directions, similar to a standard light bulb (associated with rendering methods).

Polyline: A line, shape, or surface (open or closed) created by joining arcs and lines together.

Postscript: Page description language developed by Adobe Systems, designed to handle publication-quality text, linework, fills, and bitmap images. Originally used as the printing language for Apple's LaserWriter, now has become the standard for digital printing.

Preferences: Saving one's own parameters to be used as defaults.

Quick Paint: A rendering method in modeling, which displays the surfaces of objects in in an order according to their distance from the viewer, but does not decompose intersecting surfaces, concave surfaces, and surfaces with holes. This allows it to be fast but does not always produce correct renderings. It is intended for preview level renderings.

RAM: Random Access Memory.

ROM: Read Only Memory.

Ray Tracing: An intricate rendering algorithm that can create photorealistic images. Ray tracing calculates the path of imaginary "rays" of light from an observer's viewpoint through each pixel on the surface of the object being viewed. The color for each pixel is determined by how these rays would bounce off or be absorbed into an object's surface. Ray tracing can show true reflection, refraction, transparency, or shadows. (A rendering algorithm, which determines the closest surface pixel by casting a ray from the view point through each screen pixel and intersecting it with each face. The face whose intersection point is closest to the viewer is used to calculate the pixel color. Rays which hit reflective or tranmissive surfaces are reflected or refracted according to the ray's angle of incidence and the surface normal at the intersection point. This produces renderings with accurate reflections and transparencies. Raytracing typically requires more time than other rendering algorithms, and the time it requires increases significantly when a scene contains a large number of reflective or transmissive surfaces)

Resolution: How clearly images and letters appear on a monitor screen. It also describes how clearly images and text appear on the printed page. The resolution of a monitor screen is measured in pixels. The more pixels, the higher the screen resolution and the better the picture. Printer resolution is measured in dots per inch (dpi).

SCSI: An acronym for Small Computer Serial Interface. A fast, flexible communication standard for connecting peripherals to personal computers. SCSI devices can be daisy chained to each other.

Serial Port: A serial port connects other hardware like a mouse or a printer to a computer. A serial port either can have a 9-pin or a 25-pin D connector (D-shaped).

Server: A computer that serves as a centralized resource for other computers on the network, to provide information sharing functions.

Shaded Render: A rendering method that uses z-buffer algorithm and can produce smoothly shaded surfaces, transparencies, antialiasing, and shadows from multiple lights.

Skinning: A skin object is the same as a lofted object.

Specular Reflection: A reflection parameter that determines how much of the light illuminating a surface is reflected at the incoming angle. Specular reflections typically create a "hot spot" on curved surfaces.

Spline: A term used for parametric curves. It is a smoothly curved polyline that can be either drawn directly, or derived from a control line.

Stitch: Establishing the links of reversely coincident sequences of open (unattached) segments. This operation results in two surfaces being connected into one, along open segments that coincide.

Surface Model: Three-dimensional representation of an object, defined by vertices, edges, and faces. Unlike solid models, surface models do not need to enclose a volume.

Surface Render: A rendering method in modeling that uses an algorithm known as "painter's algorithm."

Sweep Object: A sweep object is constructed through a combination of lathing and extruding. As a 2D outline is extruded along the third dimension, it can be assigned an offset distance, a rotation value, and a scaling value. Common sweep objects include springs, corkscrews, and threaded screws.

Texture Maps: A rendering algorithm which "maps" a texture image onto the surface of an object.

Transparency: A surface property that determines how much light passes through an object without being altered.

Virtual Memory: Simply refers to the disk space a computer uses as memory. Typically hard disk space which is used by a computer software program when it runs out of physical memory (RAM).

Wireframe: A representation of a three-dimensional object that shows only the lines of its contours. Wireframe is usually also a rendering mode that ignores all surface information for an object.

Z-buffer: Phong rendering with additional capabilities to show textures, bumps, shadows, backgrounds, foregrounds, transparencies, and reflections.

3

Digital Media for Architectural Design Presentation

Courtesy: Matthew Baran

Conceptual Studies

Conceptual Studies

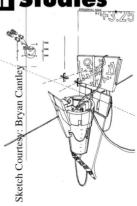

Sketch Courtesy: Bryan Cantley

CONCEPTUAL STUDIES

In an architectural design the total scope of a project involves several steps. Program, Schematic Design, Preliminary Design, Design Development, Working Drawings, Contract Document, and Construction constitutes seven identifiable stages in a total design process. At each level of these steps, a certain amount of problem solving needs to be exercised in order to achieve a satisfactory result. The process itself may be viewed in general as the activities or actions that are taken to test appropriate and alternate ideas.

The major activities involved in a creative design process deal with conceptualization, visualization, and expression of alternate ideas through two- and three-dimensional drawings, and physical three-dimensional models. The total process is an interactive one that goes back and forth with extensive cross-referencing. The interactive process of conceptualization, visualization, and expression through drawings becomes especially evident in the second, third, and fourth steps of a design activity (schematic design, preliminary design, and design development).

1. Program
2. Schematic Design
3. Preliminary Design
4. Design Development
5. Working Drawings
6. Contract Document
7. Construction

Steps 2, 3, and 4 of a design activity involve visualization.

3D computer modeling is increasingly becoming a very useful tool in all of the above three stages (visualization), but perhaps most importantly in the schematic and preliminary design phase in a total design process. The following examples in this section illustrate both commissioned and hypothetical projects that have used computer modeling techniques in the design process to study and comprehend the total design process.

Use of Conceptual 3D Model for Schematic Design Development

This project for an architecture school was developed as a dialogue between the internet (information space) and the

Microprocessor chip diagram, starting point for representation of information 'space'.

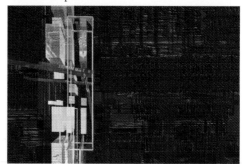

Chip diagram showing first 3-dimentional translations.

Interaction of form between original microprocessor interpretations.

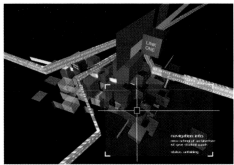

Information hub at main school level, shown during hyper-space navigation.

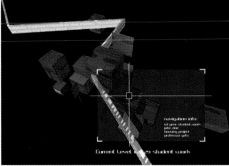

Information hub one level down, 1st year studios, shown during navigation.

physical environment (built space). The digital space was a representation of the information a traditional school of architecture would house. It borrowed many aspects of built architecture in order to define itself as 'space'. The program included areas for students and faculty, a gallery, a forum and auditorium, and a lobby. These were represented by various cubic nodes, which would dock in particular relation to one another, i.e., the gallery near the studio for virtual 'pin-ups'. These 'spaces' would be hyperlinked to one another.

A crucial element in the development of the information space was how the nodes that were not immediately 'adjacent' to one another would be traversed. A series of complex threads were necessary to accommodate the intricate locations of the nodes. These can be seen as 'search engines', similar to those we have on the internet today.

The model for a built space in turn borrowed from the information space in order to define itself. The search engine was likened to a library, since it was the element that would guide a person through the project. The information nodes had parallel built space counterparts; they housed physical equipment and information, i.e. desks, computers, drawings, instead of digital information. The collision of elements and their particular juxtapositions were maintained to achieve the relationships that were determined in the information space.

Hybrid image of information hub and model for a built school.

The outcome was an internet space which borrowed metaphors from built space, and a model for a built architecture which took queues from virtual space. This served to enhance the development of both spaces, opening up possibilities that could not have been discovered otherwise.

Courtesy:
Matthew Baran
Project: Digital Inframation Hub /
School of Architecture

013

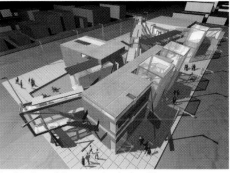

Aerial view of the new school of architecture.

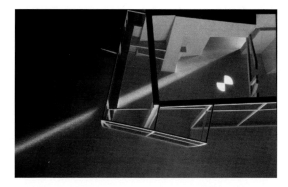

Basswood model of "phase event 01": lighting study

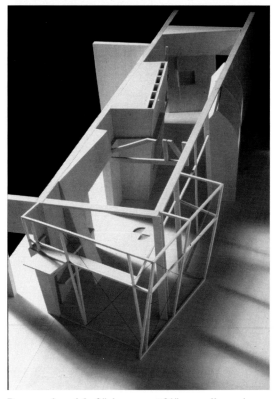

Basswood model of "phase event 01": overall massing

Use of Digital 3D Model along with Traditional Model and Sketch for Design Development Studies

Initial studies were produced through traditional hand diagrams and sketches. Chipboard and cardboard models were constructed to dimensionally explore spatial relationships. Pencil and ink drawings were executed to tighten program and component assemblies. A basswood model was produced as a "phase event." A general digital massing was then produced in Strata Studio Pro. A "phase event" digital model was constructed from the massing.

Individual components were isolated to study relationships and potentials. Existing building and site elements were removed to examine the new assemblies and their spatial implications. Hand sketches were used to further investigate problematic conditions. After the digital model was complete, images from digital models of periphery signage panels were superimposed in Photoshop to explore graphic/dimensional hybrids.

Credits:
[Form:uLA] Bryan Cantley + Kevin O'Donnell
Digital modeling assistants: Treva Kuyper, Kevin Kennedy

Cardboard study of ceiling assembly

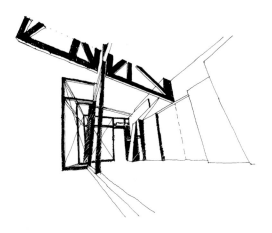

Sketch study of entry system

Digital Assembly study: progressive alternate framing systems

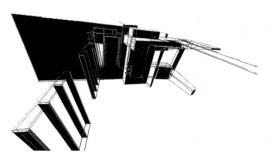

anti-cedent probe

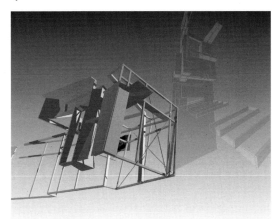

Digital Assembly study: composite of entry components and anti-cedent

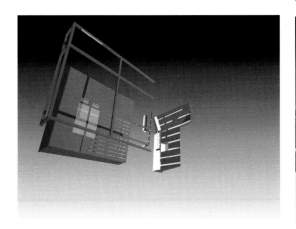

Digital Assembly study: coffee bar + second gallery entry

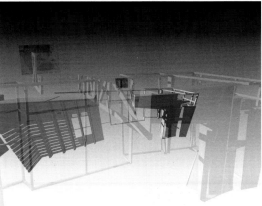

Digital Assembly study: composite of rear framing/ massing with signage

Use of Conceptual 3D Model for Study of Design Elements

The intent of these sequential models is to explain the process of manipulation and design of elements to support a specific function of the modular unit: a housing prototype is shown in this example.

The project includes developing a housing system for senior citizens and war veterans. The concept was to develop a modular system that was flexible in function as well as in formation. The final built system was curved to accommodate an odd sized lot and was composed of 52 units. The demographics of the site dictated that the majority of units were dedicated to senior citizens and war veterans. Retail units at street level were dedicated to commercial support.

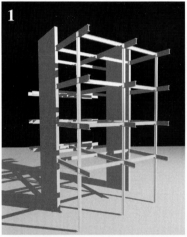

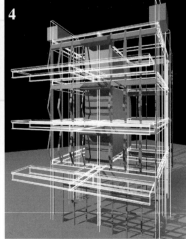

Image 1:
Rear view - Primary structure

Image 2:
Rear view - Integrated service elements

Image: 3
Rear view - Photovoltaic system integrated with privacy elements

Image: 4
Front view - Energy efficient privacy elements

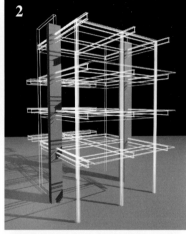

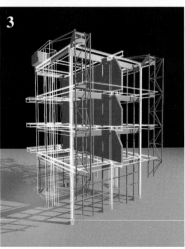

Hardware: Pentium based IBM compatible computer.

Software: AutoCAD for modeling, 3D Studio for rendering, and Photoshop for image editing

Courtesy: Warren Tamashiro
Project: Modular Unit / Housing Prototype

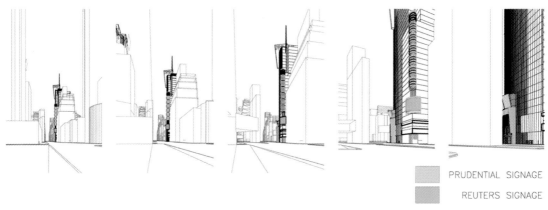

PRUDENTIAL SIGNAGE

REUTERS SIGNAGE

REUTERS BUILDING - 7TH AVENUE SIGNAGE STUDY

FOX & FOWLE ARCHITECTS 1998

Design Development Studies:

Caption: Reuters Building * 7th Avenue Signage Study. Images were created to show the clients and primary tenants * Reuters - the viability (from all 4 directions) of signage wedge which protrudes from the building face at top. Visibility and signage are two essential components to design in Times Square.

Drawing Process/Image Technique: Models were created from construction documents in AutoCAD. Photoshop used for image enhancement and correction.

Hardware: Pentium 166, 96MB RAM, Fire GL 1000 graphics card w/ 8MB VRAM

Software: AutoCAD R14, Photoshop 4.0

Project: The Reuters Building, Three Times Square, New York, New York

Courtesy: Fox & Fowle Architects, New York, New York
Digital Image Credit: Zheng Dai

Design Development Diagram

Plan Perspective Diagram

This image is a plan perspective diagram outlining the major ideas and concepts for the renovation of an existing bar and banquet room.

The use of perspective enabled the client to understand the distribution of program in plan as well as the layered spatial relationships between the various objects in three dimensions.

A hidden line rendering was generated from a 3-D model in MiniCAD and then converted to a two dimensional drawing where text and color were added.

Hardware: Apple Power Macintosh

Software: DiehlGraphisoft MiniCAD 7, Lightworks Superlite Renderer Plug-in, Adobe Photoshop.

Project: Boulevard Bistrot Banquet Room
Courtesy: Natalye Appel Architects, Houston, Texas

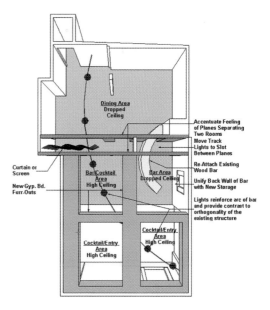

Plan Perspective Diagram

017

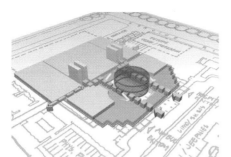

1. Building circulation as it relates to the site organization and wayfinding.

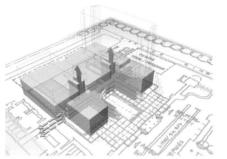

2. Circulation as the building's spine & organization of massing volumes

3. Vertical integration of the corresponding building functions

4. Bird's eye view of the campus

Design Development Studies:

The following are examples of tools used to enhance the design and planning process. The first diagram, on the top is an axonometric view of the building in relation to the site. It represents entry level circulation and major points of access for the building.

Picture 2 (left) illustrates massing, access, and circulation within a building. A diagrammatic section (picture 3) through the campus visualizes vertical integration of program elements. These concept studies are later refined into 3-dimentional image as shown in picture 4.

Computer tools such as these not only assist the project team in establishing optimum departmental relationships and circulation adjacencies but they also help to convey design ideas to the client.

All studies were done with the use of following software: AutoCAD, 3D Studio Max, and Adobe Photoshop.

Hardware:
Windows NT station with a PC based Pentium II system, 128 Mb RAM and 3D graphics accelerator card were the core hardware system for these images.

Software:
AutoCAD, 3D Studio Max, Photoshop.

Project: Philippines Medical Center, Manila, Philippines

Courtesy:
TRO/The Ritchie Organization
Design and Studies: Andrej Zarzycki

Conceptual Studies:
Form, Material, Texture, Structure, etc.

Pictures 1-5 on this page are taken from an architect's iterative process as a formal parti evolves from geometric considerations into compositional concerns involving material, surface texture, color and lighting. Digital imaging software, with tools for lighting and material mapping permits examination, evaluation and refinement of design consequences of specific combinations of architectural materials with accuracy and subtlety previously not possible.

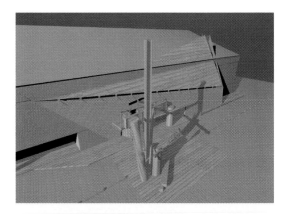

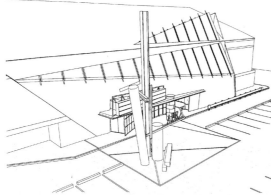

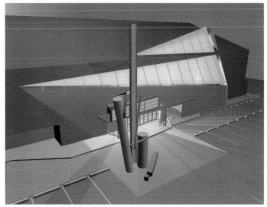

Digital study images, while they may be used in presentations, are not treated as renderings in the traditional sense. They are more akin to study models, discardable exercises the purpose of which is to facilitate decision-making.

In the imaging application, material designations can be toggled between diagrammatic/symbolic and real-world industry products with relative ease. The digital operator however, should be an experienced architect who knows what the characteristics of such real-world products actually are.

Expensive, state-of-the-art hardware is not required to create study images. These were done on PC hardware running on an Intel Pentium 133 processor with 64 MB RAM, a 4 mb graphics video accelerator, a 17-inch display and the Windows 95 operating system. Software used for these images were AutoCad 12/14, 3D Studio R4 (and Max), Adobe Photoshop.

Project: Cinema Renovation, Louisville, Kentucky
Courtesy: Richard Rauh & Associates, Atlanta, Georgia

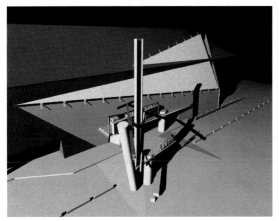

3D Model for Evolution of an Embryonic Grammar of Form

Conceptual recording of random reality and imagination. Morphosis describes, "…….Moving through Copenhagen we translate the stream of time into a frozen field of space where things and events can be assimilated we create narratives, linkages separate from our current thoughts, and manipulate that which is not present. The model represents the received frozen elements into a singular memory event which fills the meat of the brain and gives rise to the spirit of the memory. Equivalent to the brain's hippocampus, the recollection is asystematic, not a record of events waiting to be unearthed as thought by Freud. Memory, above all else, is personal and subjective. "

"…. Beyond the routine flashes of understanding, I see and see again the physical reality of the city -- some intentional, purposeful in some way, most totally random. The same place is never the same place but fragmented into always new aggregates, the consequence of collisions of other places, both interior and exterior ... sooner or later provisional. Our understanding of the flow of past life into present subverts our senses. These cubic perceptions are time made apparent, juxtaposing reality and imagination. Chronological time is disrupted-- a disruption asserting the subjectivity of our own memories and point of view, evolving an embryonic grammar of form."

Hardware and Software:
Form•Z Renderzone / Power Macintosh)

Courtesy: Morphosis
Project: HIPPOCAMPUS

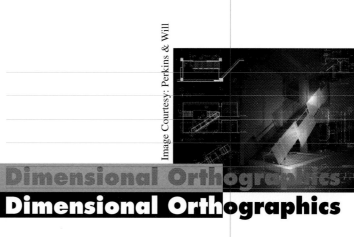

Image Courtesy: Perkins & Will

Dimensional Orthographics

DIMENSIONAL ORTHOGRAPHICS

All technical drawings are constructed on the basis of a common systems of projection. The *projection* is the relationship between a point in space and its representation on a selected plane. Depending on the nature of the projections all drawings may be divided into two basic categories: 1. multiview drawings (two-dimensional plan, elevation, and section) and 2. single-view drawings (three-dimensional axonometric and perspective).

Parallel projection and *central projection* are the two systems that are capable of portraying the three-dimensional nature of an object. *Axonometric* and *oblique* drawings fall under parallel projection (measurable), whereas *perspectives* fall under central projection (non-measurable).

A 3D computer model is capable of generating both multiview and single-view drawings from a single model. Effects of perspective views can be modified to the desired angle very simply by moving the station point and adjusting the cone of vision.

This section features a number of images that belong to the category of dimensional orthographics but either were created from a 3D model or were manipulated digitally to create a non-conventional nature of orthographics.

Dimensional CAD Drawing from 3D Model

This collage, depicting an NFL scoreboard, represents a totality of design thinking that seeks to express the tightening relationship between design process and documentation. It showcases the rigors of the trade while creating an awareness of the beauty that exists in a technical drawing.

The base data for this collage has its origins in computer 3D. First modeled in AutoCAD to assist the team in design process, it was eventually used to generate an outline for the final elevations of the scoreboard. The north elevation was isolated, stripped of its notes, given shadows, laser printed and scanned, transforming vector data into raster. The drawings experienced a loss of clarity. It was a desired effect. The image was then brought into Photoshop where it was layered with another image that still retained its notation. This latter image, scanned at an even lower resolution, was made into a negative, given transparency and cast over the first. Perspective images, represented as miniature pilot fish, were then collaged over the technical drawings in a manner that relates back to the larger manifestation.

Project: Paul Brown Stadium, Cincinnati, Ohio
Courtesy: NBBJ

Site Plan and Floor Plan
(combining raster and vector layers)

These two non-conventional site and floor plans illustrate digital integration of technical orthographic line drawing and borrowed pictorial image of colorful landscape. The plans were first drawn by hand with graphite on lithographic paper. PMT halftones of these drawings were scanned and redrawn on the computer, tracing over the original drawings in a fashion similar to inking. Unlike conventional ink drawings, the base drawing remains as a record, dissolving the distinction between process and representation. The base drawing was engaged (manipulated) as an active part of the drawing as the drawing progressed.

In these drawings, the background was made from scan 'noise' originating from a single, borrowed source. The engagement of building and site is reinforced in the drawings through the collaboration of raster and vector imaging techniques.

The drawings were made with a G3 processor in a UMAX S900. Adobe Photoshop 5 and Macromedia Freehand 8 were used in a deliberate attempt to use the computer as a drawing, rather than drafting, tool.

Courtesy: Richard Jensen, Assistant Professor
Syracuse University
Project: Itinerant Research Laboratory, Wood Buffalo National Park, Alberta and Northwest Territories, Canada.

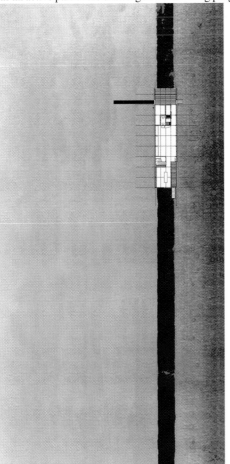

SITE PLAN
1 CLEARCUT
2 ABANDONED LOGGING ROAD
3 FOREST

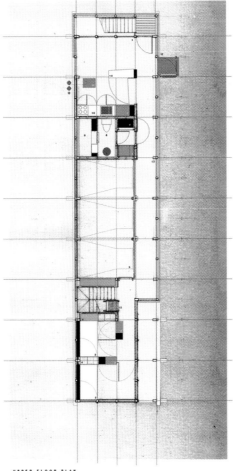

UPPER FLOOR PLAN
1 LIVING / DINING
2 FOLDOUT CHEST AND CLOSET
3 FOLDOUT BED
4 FOLDOUT DESK
5 LABORATORY BELOW / VENTS ABOVE
6 DUMBWAITER
7 DRAWERS
8 WC
9 BATHTUB
10 GALLEY
11 WOOD STOVE
12 BRIDGE
13 LADDER
14 TABLE

023

Site Plan Drawing

AutoCAD modeled site plan can effectively be converted into a conventional site plan to emphasize orthographic qualities of a two-dimensional site plan.

AutoCAD drawn site plan imported into 3D Studio to render and differentiate the surface textures of landscape features, paved surfaces, building volumes, and natural features. Shadows effectively show relative hrights of building volumes.

Hardware and Software: Intel processor based PC computer. AutoCAD with Accurender, and 3D Studio Max.

Project: Abandoibara Master Plan, Bilbao, Spain

Courtesy: Cesar Pelli & Associates, New Haven, Connecticut

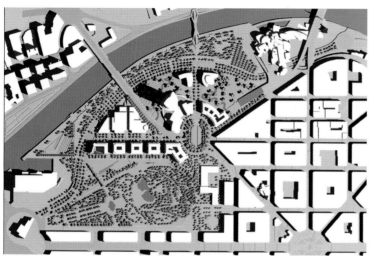

Plan-Axonometric

This jail housing pod was modeled to demonstrate and show critical lines of sight from a control officer's standpoint, thereby exposing any potential obstructions prior to construction. The use of a CADD model is superior to an actual physical model because you can be placed inside at a true eye level location. The use of this model in a demonstration with County staff resulted in several improvements in design and visibility.

Hardware and Software:
P.C. based Pentium 333 MHz 128 MB RAM. Microstation SE; Adobe Photoshop.

Project: Theo Lacy Jail Expansion - Medical Pod, Orange, California

Courtesy: HDR Architecture Inc. Dallas, Texas

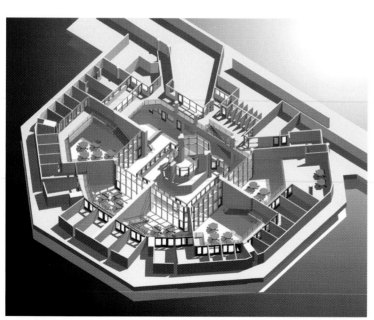

024

Section Drawing

Communicating the concept of layered volumes explored in this scheme was ideally suited to a composite approach within the drawings. While the cut plane has similar characteristics to conventional dimensional and orthographic section drawings, the depth of the image attempts to express the spatial concept in three dimensions.

Hardware: Pentium processor based networked workstations for both modeling and rendering.

Software: AutoCAD, 3D Studio, Lightscape, Photoshop.

Project: Water Treatment Lab and Administration Building, Long Beach, California

Courtesy: John Lumsden forDMJM Architects/Engineers

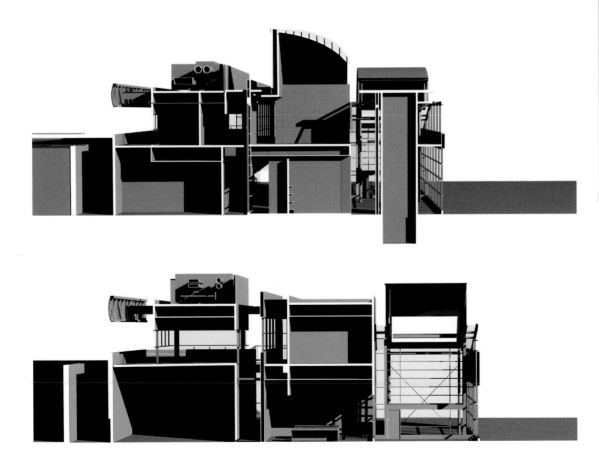

Elevation Study

The bottom mages are details of elevations, created to show the base building relationship between 3 Times Square and the existing context of nearby buildings, such as the New Victory Theatre. The challenge was to have the building read as a formidable highrise in midtown Manhattan, while being a complement to the neighborhood's older, lowrise buildings which have been preserved.

Models and elevation drawings were created from construction documents in AutoCAD. Photoshop used for image enhancement and correction.

Hardware: Pentium 166, 96MB RAM, Fire GL 1000 graphics card w/ 8MB VRAM

Software: AutoCAD R14, Photoshop 4.0.

Project: The Reuters Building, Three Times Square, New York, New York.

Courtesy: Fox & Fowle Architects, New York, New York. Digital Image: Zheng Dai and Brian Davison.

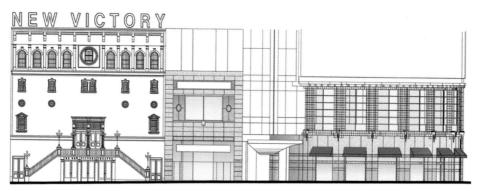

Reuters Building • South Elevation

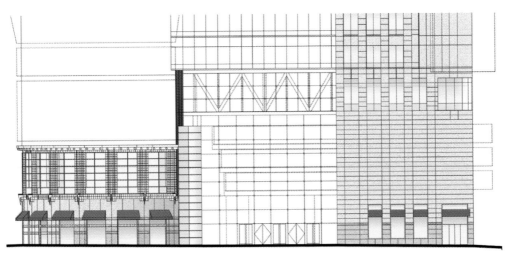

Reuters Building • East Elevation

Top: Building Base South Elevation (42nd St). Bottom: Building Base East Elevation (7th Ave)

Section Drawing
(combining raster and vector layers)

Similar to the site and floor plan drawings on page 23, the section drawing on this page illustrates techniques of combining photographic background with line drawing. The section was first drawn by hand with graphite on lithographic paper. PMT halftones of the section drawing was scanned and redrawn on the computer, tracing over the original drawing in a fashion similar to inking.

The background was made from scan 'noise' originating from a single, borrowed source. The engagement of section drawing and landscape is reinforced in the drawings through the collaboration of raster and vector imaging techniques.

The drawings were made with a G3 processor in a UMAX S900. Adobe Photoshop 5 and Macromedia Freehand 8 were used in a deliberate attempt to use the computer as a drawing, rather than drafting, tool.

Project: Itinerant Research Laboratory, Wood Buffalo National Park, Alberta and Northwest Territories, Canada.

Courtesy:
Richard Jensen, Assistant Professor
Syracuse University

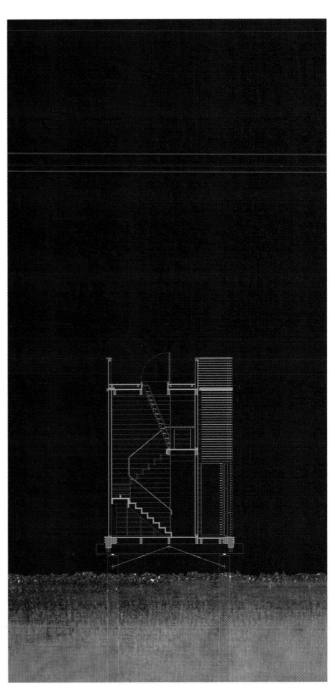

SECTION

Axonometrics

The frontal projection drawing explores the tension between wall opaqueness, translucency, and transparency as a spatial sequence from entry (north) to view beyond (south). The overall axonometric view from the northeast orchestrates the dialogue between glass panels, glass-block planes, stainless steel volumes and concrete spine-walls. The cut-away axonometric detail articulates interpenetrating interior and exterior spaces that occur at the entry system

The drawings were made with a Macintosh IIci (25MHz, 20MB). Architrion II 5.5 was used as a design development modeling tool. A technique for creating true plan obliques (axonometrics) and frontal projections was discovered by accident during the process of generating perspective views. Line weights and surface colors were manipulated with Adobe Illustrator 3.2 and rasterized with Adobe Photoshop 2.5.

Project: The Elongation House, Indian Hills, Ohio.

Courtesy: Bennett Robert Neiman, Associate Professor
University of Colorado

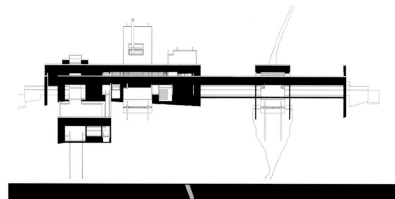

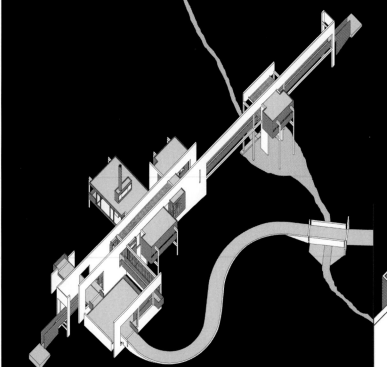

Composite Dimensional Orthographics and Rendered Perspective

This composite image of a 'Connecting Stair' documents cleverly both dimensional multiview orthographics and a single-view rendered perspective, and expresses the relationship between design aesthetic and technical detailing capabilities in one digital image. The drawing documents dimensional plan, section , elevation, and details as a separate layer on top of a rendered perspective layer. The spot light used in the rendering not only highlights the material, reflection, and refraction of the surfaces but also creates a contrast background for other two-dimensional drawings to be read in reverse.

Each of the 2-D details shown on that image were imported into Photoshop from the actual CAD construction drawing details and were composed within the image in the approximate area they occur in relation to the stair.

The 3D model of the stair was constructed from AutoCAD line drawing, then imported into 3DstudioMax where modeling and material studies were developed until the concept was fine-tuned. Camera angles and lighting effects were selected and the final model was rendered and then imported into Photoshop where contrast and color balancing was applied with other 2D drawings.

Hardware: Pentium 266 PC
Software: 3D Studio Max, AutoCAD r.13, Adobe Photoshop

Project: Connecting Stair, Perot Systems Corporation, Cambridge MA

Courtesy: Perkins & Will
Images: Jason Rosenblatt

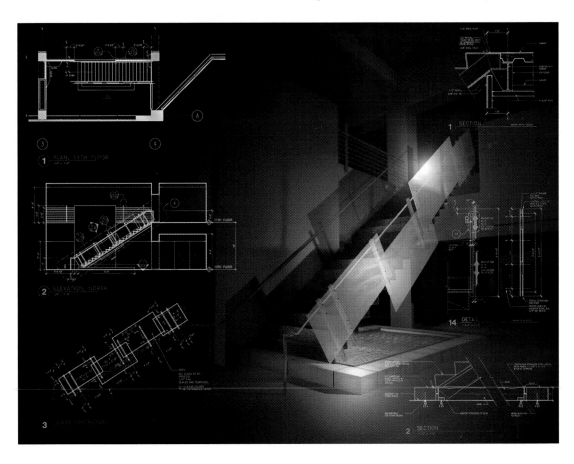

Plan and Elevation

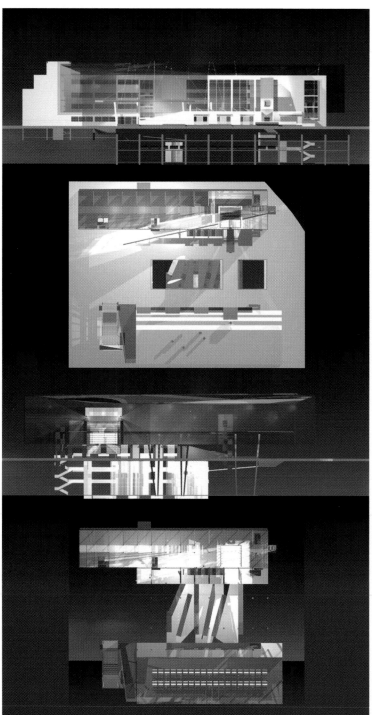

The elevations and plans shown here document the Velaspace Prototype images on page 65. Laminated-textured glass and photovoltaic cells describe translucent and reflective surfaces. The attenuated structural elements further express the lightness and thinness of a newly considered architectural field enhancing the implementation of self-sustaining, energy efficient construction techniques and innovations. Lighting effects in Form•Z and Photoshop were used to enhance the ephemeral quality of the proposed materials. Plans and elevations developed in Form•Z were exported to Photoshop where they were collaged into a common ground plane. Solar flares, screens and color matching enhanced the luminosity of the orthographic documentation beyond conventional drafting techniques.

Hardware: Macintosh PowerMac 9600/300, 4 GB/128 RAM. Macintosh G3/266, 4 GB/128 RAM. HP Printers & Plotters.

Software: Form•Z 2.9.3, Photoshop 4.0, PageMaker 6.0.

Project: Velaspace Prototype
Courtesy: Barbara Ambach, Architect
College of Architecture and Planning
University of Colorado at Denver.

030

3D Modeling and Rendering

3D Modeling and Rendering

Images: Author

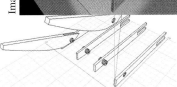

3D MODELING AND RENDERING

Modeling

Constructing and composing objects in a three-dimensional computer environment having length, width and depth is usually referred as 3D modeling.

3D Solids (solid models) and 2D surface objects (surface models) are the two basic types of models that are used to create three-dimensional objects in a computer environment. Solid models are analogous to solid foam, wood, or clay physical models, whereas surface models are analogous to paper or cardboard physical models. Most modeling applications also provide a set of three-dimensional primitives (cubes, cones, cylinders, etc.) that can be transformed either in their geometry, their topology, or both to create the desired object.

Unique three-dimensional elements can also be constructed by rotating, sweeping and meshing two-dimensional elements.

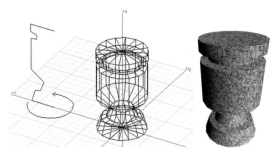

Object created with 360-degree rotation of a line element

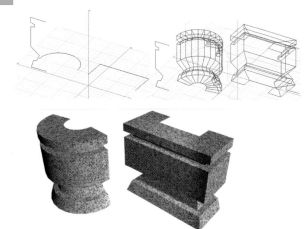

Same line element to create object with sweep along paths

Rendering

The techniques used to create images that are more realistic than straightforward line drawings can be grouped under the general heading of rendering. At its simplest, this may require nothing more than removing hidden lines to give the illusion of three dimensions. At the other extreme is the goal of "photo-realism" or the production of a synthetic digital image indistinguishable from a digital photograph.

A wide range of rendering techniques that are available and used frequently can be divided into the following categories of visibility, illumination, shading, and lighting.

VISIBILITY
• Hidden-line algorithms
• Hidden-surface algorithms (Backface cull, Depth sort/painter's algorithm, Z-buffer)

ILLUMINATION
• Ambient
• Lambertian
• Phong

SHADING
• Flat
• Smooth, Gouraud
• Phong (Surface mapping, shadows)
• Ray tracing (Reflection, refraction, atmospheric effects)
• Radiosity (Soft shadows, inter-object illumination)

IMAGE CHARACTERISTICS
• Shadow casting
• Reflection
• Transparency
• Refraction

LIGHTING
• Type (Parallel, Point, Distributed)
• Location
• Orientation
• Intensity
• Chromatic content

ELEMENTS OF RENDERING:
• Geometrical Characteristics
• Object Characteristics (Color, Roughness, Texture, Transparency)

• Light Source and Shadow
(Ambient, Direct)
• Atmospheric and environmental
effects

For any modeling and rendering
undertaking it is important to
consider the following points:

• Time available
• Levels of complexity
• Nature of the geometrical model
• Software and hardware capability
• Quality of rendering required

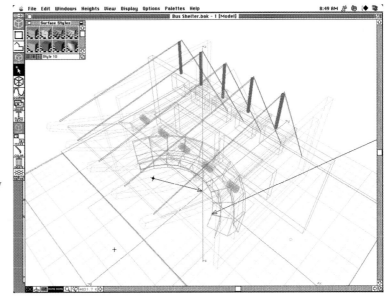

Images on this page and next two pages illustrate a proposal for a University Bus Stop, modeled and rendered in
form•Z Renderzone.

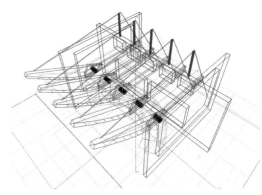

Wireframe

The model was created in the 3D mode of the application
as a schematic design and dimensional accuracy was not
critical to the model. Basic operations used to create the
model include creating solid vertical walls and inserting
openings, creating two-dimensional shapes in elevation
with polyline and extruding or adding depth perpendicular to the surface, inserting hole on three-dimensional objects, sweeping line element along a defined path, moving
individual objects both in plan and elevation, creating and
moving multiple copies of a created three-dimensional
object, rotating objects both in plan and elevation.

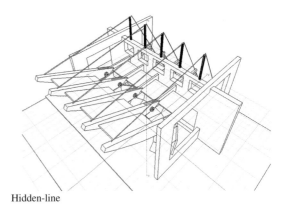

The top image is a screen shot of the wireframe model
with the modeling tools and surface style palette. Bottom
two images are wireframe and hidden line views of the
same model.

Hidden-line

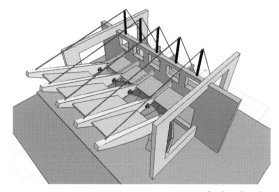

Surface Render
(Quick Shade)

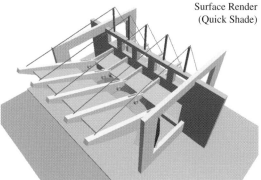

Shaded Render
(Flat Shade)

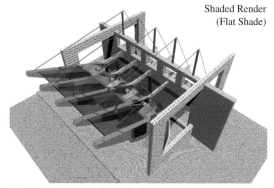

Form•Z Renderzone (combination of Z-Buffer and ray trace)

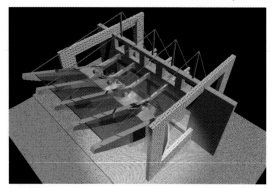

Renderzone with additional cone light source

Images on this page show various rendering effects created in form•Z Renderzone. All images were saved as individual Tiff files and imported into Photoshop to resize them for this page layout.

The following are the different levels of rendering modes that can be found in a quality modeling-rendering application.

Wireframe: Objects are drawn with a series of lines. Outlines are drawn without indication of surfaces.

Hidden Line: Produces a rendering of wireframe objects, but with surfaces implied by the removal of hidden lines.

Quick Paint: This rendering method displays the surfaces of objects in an order according to their distance from the viewer, but does not decompose intersecting surfaces, concave surfaces, and surfaces with holes. This allows it to be fast but does not always produce correct renderings. It is intended for preview level renderings.

Quick Shade: This mode produces an image with simple shaded objects. In addition to showing object surfaces, lighting direction and the resulting shading of objects is calculated. This is a simple surface rendering, using only one lighting calculation per face.

Flat Shade: Each face of the object is rendered as a single, opaque, surface in a uniform color.

Gouraud: In this mode the objects are rendered smooth, where the color at given pixel on a face is averaged from the colors at the corner points of the face. This shading method adds a degree of realism to a scene, but is not able to generate highlights on curved surfaces.

Phong: Phong rendering is a light-oriented algorithm, with the capability to render smooth surfaces, reflectivity (environments only), shadows, transparency, and surface maps. This method allows for the generation of specular highlights on curved surfaces.

Raytrace: This mode creates enhanced photo-realistic images with true reflectivity, shadows, refraction, transparency, etc. This rendering method calculates how rays of light react to object surfaces within the model before reaching the viewer's eye.

Z-Buffer: A variation of Phong rendering with additional capabilities to show textures, bumps, shadows, backgrounds, foregrounds, transparencies, and reflections.

Radiosity: This rendering method considers the effects of inter-reflections among objects. This mode produces images of unparalleled realism.

034

Images show sequential process of creating and rendering primary components of the Bus Stop model using form•Z Renderzone.

For the wedge-shaped element shown to the right, two-dimensional face was drawn first in elevation using polyline. Extrusion depth perpendicular to the surface was given to create the 3D object. Similarly the other rectangular bar was created from two-dimensional elevation. 'Insert Hole' command was used to create circular holes. After the rectangular bar and the wedge-shaped bar were joined together with the pivot pin, rotation command was used for the wedge-shaped object to place it in its relative desired position. Switching between 3D plane and 2D plane/s confirmed the desired proportions and locations of the created objects. Multiple copies were made to create five of these elements to construct the structure of the roof. Material and surface style was chosen from the 'Surface Style Palette,' and reflectiveness was added for rendering.

The brick wall was drawn in plan and extruded vertically upward to its desired height. 'Insert Opening' command was used to create rectangular openings on the wall. 'Brick' was chosen from the 'Surface Style Palette' for the rendering of the wall.

Both glass surfaces were drawn in plan with its extrusion depth and moved to their proper position using 'Move' and 'Rotation' command. Transparency, and reflectiveness were added to the glass material for rendering. For final rendering additional 'Cone Light' was used with shadow option.

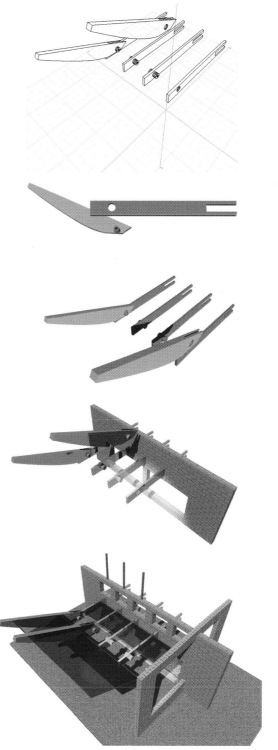

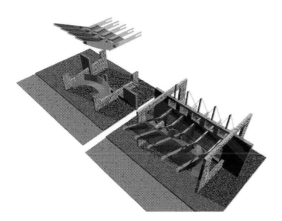

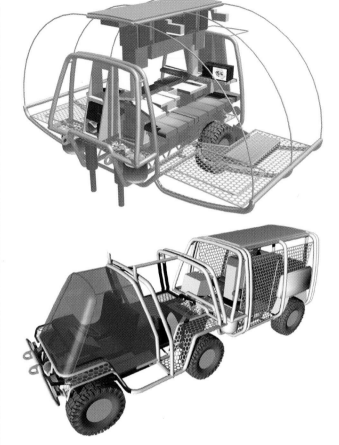

Modeling and Rendering Material

These images illustrate a concept study for a multi-purpose commercial off-road vehicle. The commercial vehicle could function in capacities such as a mobile ranger station for use in the national park system or other similar uses. The vehicle concept was conceived as a modular design consisting of a tractor or power plant and a plug-on special-function module. The plug-on special-function modules can have various functions. In the residential version, fold-up seats fit together to form a cot or bench seat flanking a "core" island which contains fold-out table, sink, refrigerator and storage space. The side walls consist of expanded metal decking mounted on curved frames which fold down on deployment of the module. When the walls fold down the decking becomes flooring, the roof pops up and canvas curved sidewalls are supported by flexible aluminum tubular supports.

Primary hardware used were RS-6000 workstation and Power Macintosh. Output devices include Pictrography color digital printer, vector / rastor electrostatic plotter and laser printers. CATIA and Form•Z were used for modeling, Renderzone and Strata Studio Pro for rendering and animations.

Project: Qamel Speciality Vehicle
Courtesy: A. Scott Howe

Translucency in Rendering Material

This image, typical of a work-in-progess, is a section perspective of a world Cup Stadium proposal for the city of Sapporo, Japan. It shows the upper concourse and its relationship to the spectator seating area of the event. The image is skeletal while subtly informing us of surfaces by rendering them with a translucent quality. This technique creates a sense of volume while retaining enough technical information to illustrate its relationship to the grander vision. Computer model and rendering were accomplished using Alias software on an SGI station.

Project: Sapporo World Cup Stadium Competition Entry
Courtesy: NBBJ

Materiality and Light in Rendering

This image, a Form•Z "Renderzone" rendering, demonstrates very clearly intended materiality, surface texture, and light and shadow. The modeling and rendering software was used to study different positions of the sun throughout the year and day to position building form and apertures to shape the experience of adopting an animal with natural light. Generated in a PowerMacIntosh CPU, the image is a full raytraced rendering from a computer model.

Project: Charlottesville Society for the Prevention of Cruelty to Animals (lobby interior), Charlottesville, Virginia
Courtesy: MAZE Design Collaborative, Inc.
John and Linda Maze

037

Rendering Projection Light

This 3D Rendered image from 3D Studio Max for an auditorium interior show the intention and quality of interior space while the projection is running. To create the effect of running projection and lighting condition inside the space volumetric light source projecting an image was used. Rendered image was then saved as BMP and imported into Photoshop. Using the lens flare effect the glow was given to the projection light source.

Courtesy: Stephen J. Spikes, Sheffield, England

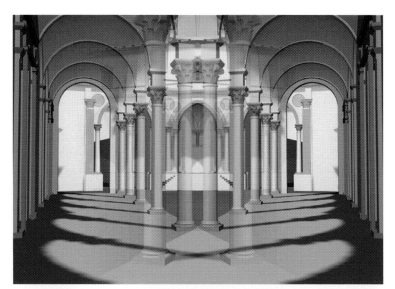

Materiality, Light and Surrealistic Space

These two images explore the architectural boundary of the possible with the impossible. By twisting reality during design, Andrzej Zarzycki transforms original spaces into surrealistic spaces. Experimentation with elements of light, texture and materials frequently may lead to imaginary worlds of pure exploration and virtual environments.

Work was produced on a Windows NT station with a PC based Pentium II system, 128 MB of RAM and 3D graphic accelerator cards. Softwere used were Lightscape/Light® from Discreet Logic and AutoCad from AutoDesk. Adobe Photoshop and Premiere were used for the image and animation editing.

Project: Variations on theme of Renaissance
Courtesy: Andrzej Zarzycki

Site Plan Showing Lighting Intent

The purpose of these two images was to show the level of illumination along the proposed routes and existing public transport routes to upgrade the circulation route and illumination condition. Top image shows location plan showing the proposal in context during day light. The bottom image shows upgraded illumination condintion after dark.

Two-dimensional survey plan scanned as a bitmap image to create 3D site model by using extrusion. Contours at the groundplane were traced using spline curves and connected with mesh to create final site ground. It was exported into 3D Studio Max as a 3DS file, and textured for rendering effect. The intensity of the default light was reduced to create the night effect and additional source lights along the roads were added to upgrade the existing illumination conditions. Source lights were further enhanced by retouching in Photoshop.

Pentium processor based computer and AutoCAD14, 3D Studio Max 1.2., Phtoshop 4.0 were used for hardware and software

Project: Picture Box Cinema, Sheffield, England.
Courtesy: Stephen J. Spikes, Sheffield, England

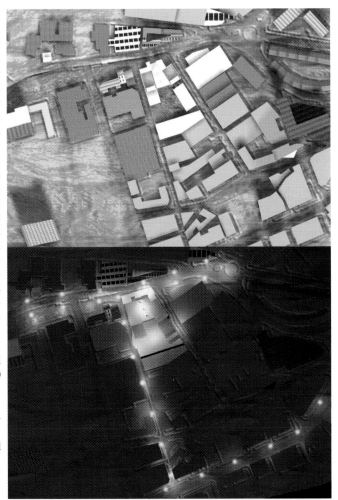

039

Adding Sketchy Effects

In this image filtered sketchy effect in the site plan highlights the proposed building (at this point in its shematic stage) from existing ones.

3D Rendered images from 3D Studio Max were saved as BMP and imported into Photoshop. Sketchy lines were drawn to add relevant details into a copy of the original image. Specific areas of the copied image were selected and a filter (charcoal and chalk) was applied to create further effects. The final image is a combination of both images using the manipulation of transparency on the filtered image.

Courtesy: Stephen J. Spikes, Sheffield, England

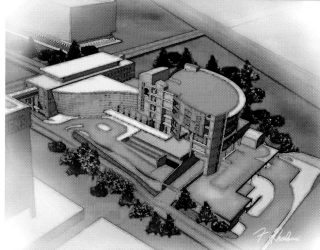

040

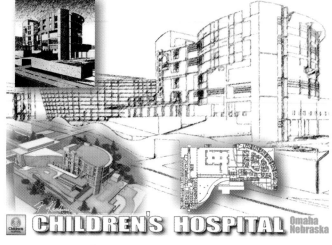

Image Manipulation

The following digital images assist display techniques in achieving an artistic and impressionistic flavor from a computer rendered image for presentation purposes. In the past architects avoided using computer images for presentation because of the rigid look of the image. Usually in the early stages of design it is preferred to give a feeling of design in sketches rather than a cold approximation photorealistic computer image. Today several programs offer an alternative option for creating a hand drawn sketchy look from any raster images.

TrueSpace was used to generate multiple 3D images at different views for visualization (pictures 1&3). The aerial view was brought into the Adobe Photoshope 5.0 and multiple filters were applied (picture 2) to simulate a traditional art look and feeling. The image was first saved as JPG low compression to get a blocky and rough-edged look, then saved back as a TIF for further manipulation. Multiple artistic filters such as "Paint Daubs" and "Watercolor" at different settings were applied on one image while in Photoshop.

Picture 3 shows multiple images juxtaposed to create a dynamic sheet composition. Each image was produced in the same fashion as explained above. The background line drawing was generated by using the "Find Edge" filter to create a line work out of a raster image. Then color was changed to black and white and back to green to keep a consistent color line drawing. While in Photoshop "Rough Pastel" was used to create brush strokes and convey texture on line. The line quality changed from a straight line computer generated to a rough hand drawn sketchy look. A typical floor plan was superimposed with a drop shadow to stand out and float against the background.

Hardware and Software: PC based Pentium II - 200 MHz 128 MB RAM. Microstation SE, TrueSpace 3.1 - Caligari, Adobe Photoshop.

Project: Childrens Hospital

Courtesy: HDR Architecture Inc. Omaha, NE
Computer Images: Farzan. Kholousi

Adding Foreground Effects

The AutoCAD generated mesh is rendered with background sky and over a flat mirror element in Max software and then placed as the background layer in Adobe Photoshop. Further correcting the brightness-contrast-intensity enhances the quality of the rendered image. Next the clipped images as sequentially shown in the layer arrangement from top left corner are added over the background master image. Copying the clipped images and flipping them horizontally in different layer creates the reflections of the clipped images on water. Then their transparency is increased.

Project: Unique Promenade Apartment, Dhaka, Bangladesh

Courtesy: VISTAARA Architects, Dhaka, Bangladesh
Digital Rendering: Mustapha Khalid, M. Foyezullah

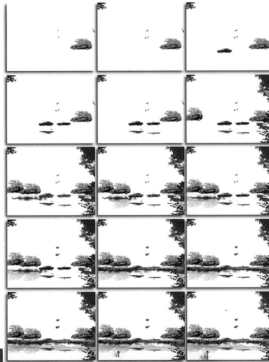

Digital Architecture

Adding Background

The building is generated basically by the help of AutoCAD and the moldings, columns and other ornamental elements were keyed in 3D Studio 2 Loft and then added to the mesh. A scanned image of the palm tree is placed as the background layer in Adobe Photoshop and the clipped image of 3D model is then placed over it. To achieve depth other clipped-scanned-images of trees and car are placed over the building layer.

Project: Domus Residence, Dhaka, Bangladesh

Courtesy: VISTAARA Architects, Dhaka, Bangladesh
Digital Rendering: Mustapha Khalid, M. Foyezullah

Adding Entourage

The vehicles in the foreground in this image are a blend of 3D and 2D elements. All the three wheelers and the Chevy are keyed in 3D and other cars and people are pasted from clipped image in different layers as required. The hedges in the verandah and in front of the building are directly drawn with paint tool in Adobe Photoshop

Project: Charuneer Apartment, Dhaka, Bangladesh

Courtesy: VISTAARA Architects, Dhaka, Bangladesh
Digital Rendering: Mustapha Khalid, M. Foyezullah

042

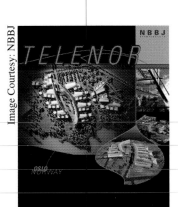

Desktop Formats

Desktop Formats

DESKTOP PUBLISHING FORMATS

Desktop applications are usually referred as page layout programs. A page layout software's strength is its extensive importing and linking capabilities to organize text, graphics, spreadsheets, charts, movie frames, and other file formats from various popular programs. Such applications are tools for creation of a variety of publications, from newsletters and brochures to color catalogs and magazines. All effective desktop applications support a large selection of file formats, which lets one easily import text and graphics from various sources. Usually they provide capabilities that make printing and prepress work easier.

Typographic controls and page design capabilities and import capabilities are the important features of a good desktop publishing program. Although there are a large number of software oackages available in the market, 'Pagemaker' and 'QuarkXpress' are the two applications that became standard choices for graphic designers and professional printers.

Graphic Poster (Bottom image)

This graphic poster documents the basic concept of the Amgen Data Center project (a massive cosmetic and structural renovation of an existing concrete tilt-up building) by emphasizing various components of the building along with texts in one composite image.

AutoCad based plans, sections, and elevations were imported into Form•Z and Adobe Illustrator where they were transformed into 3D models and graphic images. Computer models were montaged in Photoshop with site photographs. Graphic "posters" were assembled in Adobe Illustrator.

Hardware: IBM compatible Pentium 200 MHz, 96 MB RAM, Diamond Stealth graphics card, 17" NEC monitor
Software: AutoCAD Release 13, Form•Z Renderzone v. 2.9, Adobe Photoshop 4.0, Adobe Illustrator 6.0

Project: AMGEN Building 10 Data Center, Thousand Oaks, California
Courtesy: SMP-SHG Architects
Carl Hampson Project Designer

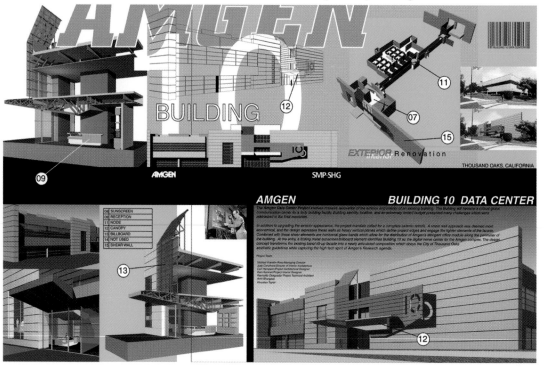

■ Digital Architecture

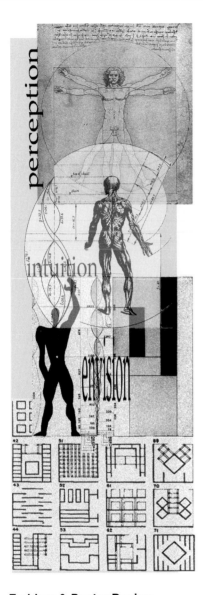

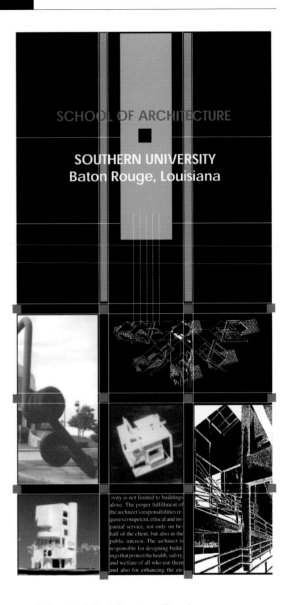

Emblem & Poster Design
Forum at the Crossroads - 1997 ACSA National Conference

Sketches, well-known architectural icons and text were screened to various opacities and superimposed in Photoshop. The final emblem was then exported to QuarkXpress for formatting and output.

Hardware: PowerMac 9600/300
Software: Photoshop 4.0 and QuarkXPress 3.3

Courtesy: Barbara Ambach, Architect. College of Architecture and Planning, University of Colorado at Denver.

School of Architecture Brochure
Southern University, Baton Rouge, Louisiana

Pen and ink drawings, photographs, and text composed in PageMaker for layout. Electronic file sent to a professional printer for final printing in 2-color.

Hardware: Power Macintosh 8500/132, HP ScanJet 3C, HP LaserJet 5MP.
Software: DeskScan, Microsoft Word, PageMaker.

Courtesy: M. Saleh Uddin

Abstract of a Project

This particular image is intended to be an abstract of a project, a diagrammatic, multi-directional map intended to motivate the viewer (as well as the designers) toward further discourse and innovation. Response and counter-response based on project agendas provide the conceptual framework for image derivation. Completed renderings from Form•Z, line drawings from Microstation, vector images from Illustrator and text from QuarkXPress are imported into Photoshop. The images are then manipulated, layered, and ingrained to reflect a particular bias.

Hardware: Power Macintosh 8500/120, 144 MB RAM, 3-GB hard disk, Iomega Zip 100.
Software: Adobe Photoshop, Form•Z Radiosity, Microstation SE, QuarkXPress, and Adobe Illustrator.

Project: 82120-1597:3nightclub, Charlotte North Carolina.
Courtesy: kevinkennedy/terryvickers, Charlotte North Carolina.

Display Board

This image was produced for marketing purposes. The final product was a large format board that was used for traveling displays. It showcases a project in an exciting manner and generates hype for the firm's services. The individual images, created in 3D Studio Max using a Form•Z model are collaged with text in Adobe Illustrator.

Competition entry for Mok Dong Retail/Entertainment Complex, Seoul, Korea.
Courtesy: NBBJ.

Postcards / Greetings Cards

RE:4A

IN
COLLABORATION
WITH
GLENN RESCALVO
DESIGN STUDIO

PAUL WARCHOL
PHOTOGRAPHY

SIMINT
SHOWROOM

NO. 9303

NEW YORK
NY

1994

These images were created
and professionally printed
specifically as postcards
intended for distribution to
clients and colleagues.

Top Postcard:
This postcard was pro-
duced using PageMaker on
the Macintosh. After deter-
mining which photograph
of the project would be incorporated, a layout was
produced coordinating text
and images.

RESOLUTION: 4 ARCHITECTURE

Season's
Greetings

Bottom Postcard:
The 6"x4" postcard is a
desktop layout produced in
QuarkXpress on the
Macintosh. Various 3D
models of this 'House for
a Roofer' in Long Island,
New York, were digitally
imported in QuarkXPress
and composed with text for
a prepress file format.

Courtesy: Resolution: 4
Architecture, New York,
New York

048

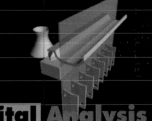

Digital Analysis

Digital Analysis

DIGITAL ANALYSIS

An analysis is an abstract process of simplification that reduces a total work into its essential elements. In architectural analysis the primary goal of a design analysis is to expose the underlying concept, organizational pattern, and execution process of the whole system through simplified diagrams, sketches, or models.

In order to focus on architectural organizational strategy a diagrammatic method of analysis may be used which dissects the primary form/s in order to show how the various elements are related to each other and to particular issues. This kind of dissection highlights certain underlying aspects of the organization, seeking to discover the theme of the work.

An act of analysis can occur at any ot the following three stages :

1. Predesign stage (research, theories, concept formation)
2. During design (formulation of architectonic means and organizational strategies)
3. After design (understanding a built work by separating components from the whole)

Digital 3D drawings particularly may become very useful in such an analysis because of their versatility of both diagrammatic and three-dimensional nature in communicating the main idea in a straightforward manner. With the additional capabilities of light, color, and material texture in the digital media, the representation of analysis can significantly be more effective. Perhaps the most advanced analysis technique in the digital media would be to formulate a digital multimedia representational method that takes into account various digital techniques (including multimedia and hypermedia) to create an interactive environment to illustrate analysis of precedents of architecture or a future design proposal.

Representation of an analysis involves processing the drawing in to following categories:

• Simplification
• Emphasis
• Reduction (Morphological Reduction, Typological Reduction)
• Addition (Geometric System, Function and Use)
• Explosion / assemblage
• Contrast in Graphics
• Hierarchy in Graphic Representation

ISSUES FOR ANALYSIS
All analyses may be grouped under the following categories, and each category may have several subdivisions:

1) Natural features/factors/qualities
2) Physical elements/factors/qualities
3) Aesthetic features/factors/qualities
4) Cultural features/factors/qualities
5) Social elements/factors/qualities
6) Visual features/factors/qualities
7) Perceptual features/qualities
8) Climatic factors
9) Circulation

The following topics are only a few of the many issues to be considered for a building analysis:

A. CONTEXT
• Location, site, and contextual relationship • Site forces
• Approach route • Movement route • Microclimate

B. BASIC UNDERSTANDING
• Design principles • Figure / Ground • Parti diagram
• Zones • Circulation sequence (entry-space-exit) •
Surrounding structures • Spatial flow

C. VISIBLE COMPONENTS
• Form/Mass/Volume/Shape/Space • Cluster of units •
Mass penetrated • Containment • Volumes against membrane/frame etc. • Geometrical adaptation •
Structure • Grid and frames • Facades/Facade themes/
Fenestration • Envelope • Enclosure • Layers • Planes •
Solid/Void • Horizontal/Vertical features

D. PRINCIPLES/SYSTEMS
• Composition of form, space, and techniques • Proportions in plan, section, elevation • Geometric order: rhythm, repetition • Light, color, shade, and shadow
• Transformation: Functional, Formal, Spatial, and Elemental • Axes • Core • Datum • Regulating lines
• Equilibrium/Hierarchy • Thematic modulation •
Addition/Subtraction • Contrast • Tension • Interlock

E. LEVELS OF PERCEPTION (PERCEPTUAL)
• Dynamism • Visual shock • Aesthetic • View and vista
• Variety and drama • Seasonal changes

Visible Components of Analysis in a Cube

Mass

Solid / Void

Core

Solid / Void

Unit / Whole

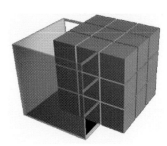

Volume / Membrane

Repetitive / Unique

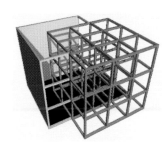

Frame / Membrane

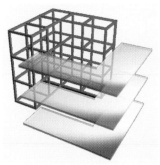

Skeletal / Planer

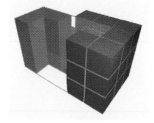

Subtraction

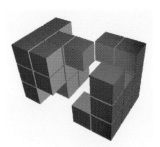

Interlock

Subtraction

Layer

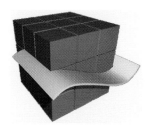

Mass Penetrated

Layer

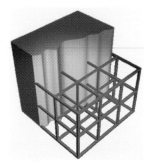

Frame / Mass

Envelope / Core

Facade / Mass

Datum

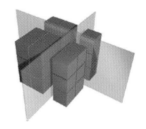

Axis

Offset

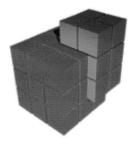

Addition

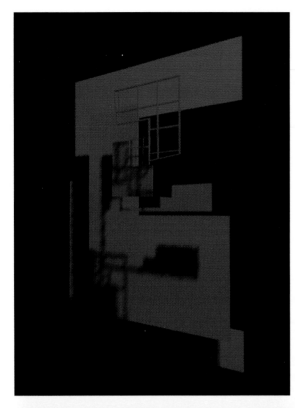

Analysis of Building Form

The use of computer modeling software to model architectural form in a unique way is pursued in this example of a student project. The project involves the student teams researching a building with complex and involved formal qualities, and then performing spatial analysis of an important view. In this case the study is based on the Koizumi Office Building by Peter Eisenman. Rather than merely building a replica of an existing building, the students study key formal components to the design and build interpretations/descriptions of those forms in a series of extracted layers. The layers are attributed with a material, lighting elements are introduced, and shadows cast. Each of these attributes extends the understanding of the formal relationships and logic. The intention is to neutralize the rest of the content; and simply study the form. Form is visible and spatial, key attributes to which the computer modeling is particularly well suited.

The models were created in 3D Studio. The shapes were built in 2D Shaper as individual files, then lofted in 3D Lofter to give the layers a slight depth for increased rendering quality. After each shape is built, they are all combined into a final file. This final file is created, a single spotlight is added, and a simple plastic material is assigned to the shapes. A camera view is then created and the renderings are built.

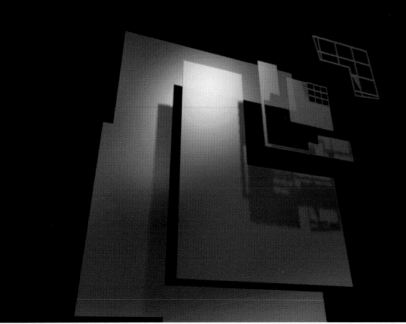

Hardware: 486PCs, 16MB RAM
Software: 3D Studio

Courtesy: Keelan P. Kaiser, Adjunct Asst. Professor
University of Nebraska-Lincoln
Images: Nick Benjamin and Glen Stach

Study of 'Sight-lines" in a Site Plan

These drawings (part of a series) were born out of an experimental analysis in which certain difficulties were evident in resolving the spatial relationships of the site layout. The resultant process was both stimulating and unconventional, working beyond the orthodox principles of architectural drawing and innovating within the scope of the design processes.

A series of vertical layers of plans ("force planes") rendered in progressive luminosity and translucency in AutoCAD and 3D StudioMax intends to produce a lucid and cogent spatial analysis for an urban project. Through the mode of translucency hidden patterns could thus emerge and be read in parallel within the existing site fabric.

Utilizing the original AutoCAD site plan as the basis, the drawing was digitized and then given depth by modeling in 3D. The model was then rendered, using plain and neutral colors for the general environment and the lofted 3D shapes. The projected "force planes" were rendered using a type of frosted, semi-translucent glass. These in turn were given a luminescence that would highlight their presence and contextual affect.

Hardware: Pentium processor based PC.

Software: AutoCAD and 3D Studio Max.

Courtesy: Zareen Mahfooz Rahman, Sheffield, England
Project Title: Space-Form analysis schematic

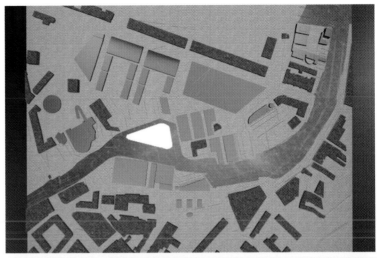

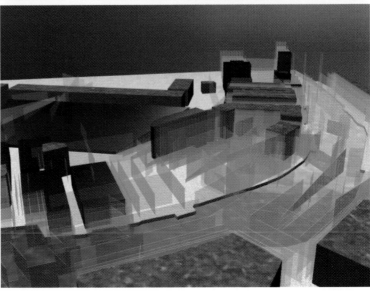

Study of Proportions

Golden section diagram drawn on top of plan and elevation to study Le corbusier's use of golden section proportion in Villa Savoye.

A 3D model was created in MiniCAD and views of plan and elevation were saved as individual files. Using the main walls of the plan, and important vertical lines of the elevation as the primary generator of the proportional system in both plan and elevation golden section diagram was su-

perimposed on top of the orthographic drawing. Golden section: a/b = b/(a+b)

Hardware:Pentium 133MHz PC and Power Macintosh 7200 with a Zip drive.

Software: MiniCAD 7.0, and Photoshop.

Courtesy: Yoshitaka Mishima
University of Sheffield, Sheffield, England

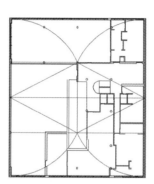

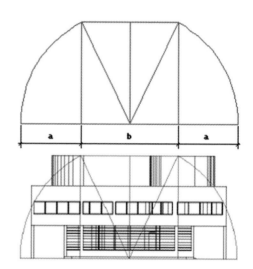

Distance relationship, cone of vision and amount of details

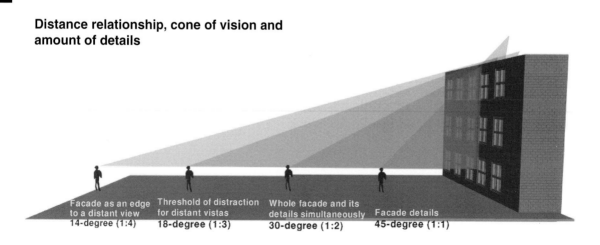

Facade as an edge to a distant view
14-degree (1:4)

Threshold of distraction for distant vistas
18-degree (1:3)

Whole facade and its details simultaneously
30-degree (1:2)

Facade details
45-degree (1:1)

Configuration Analysis of an Urban Area
District of Narmak, Tehran, Iran
(Use of Space Syntax Software)

"Space Syntax" theory and techniques which has been developed in University college of London are the best methodology for the configuration analysis of spaces in buildings and urban areas. It analyzes all parts of the system in relation to all other parts. Space syntax has formed the basis for a new generation of software programs through which computer modelling has become both interactive and dynamic.

Space syntax software is able to analyze the shape of settlements through an abstract model. This abstract model is called an axial map. It consists of a network of axial lines that represent how far observers can have an uninterrupted impression of visibility and permeability as they move about towns and look from distance in various directions.

The computer analysis of the axial map produces two kinds of outputs; numerical data in the form of line number with spatial parameters assigned to each and graphic data in the form of maps in which lines are colored up according to their value on the various parameters. The parameters' values of lines are represented by the color of spectrum from red for most integrated and dark blue for most segregated lines.

The core concept of the space syntax analysis is integration. It is proven that the higher the value of integration of the space, the higher density of activity - especially movement - within the space. As the integration value decreases, the density of movement also decreases. Therefore the graphic presentation of this software allows the designer to acknowledge the heart of the city and roles of its various parts.

Any intervention within the city would have an effect on all parts of the city. Space Syntax software enable us to visualize these subtle changes. Analysis of the three stages of development of the Old Quarter of Yazd in hot arid region of Iran is an example of the ability of the software to highlight the more complicated aspects of design. Figure 1 is the base map of the Old Quarter of Yazd. Figures 2, 3 and 4 show the integration analysis of the development stages of the city.

As the axial analysis of the walled city (figure 2) of Yazd shows, at this stage, the most integrated parts of the city were the thoroughfares, which lay between gates. They facilitated access to important places within the city such

Figure 1: Base map of the Old Quarter of Yazd, Iran.

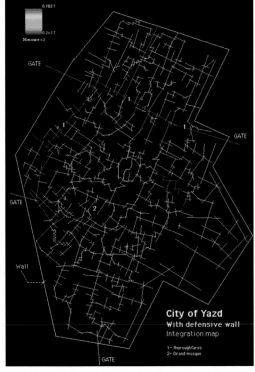

Figure 2: City of Yazd with defensive wall.

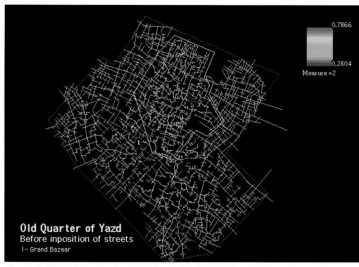

Figure 3: Development beyond the defensive wall.

Drawing Process / Digital Technique: Lines were drawn to represent streets and spaces. Then the line drawn map was scanned and imported to MiniCAD and each line was drawn again. MiniCAD file was exported and saved as a PICT imag. PICT image was brought into 'Axman', a configuration analysis software developed by School of Bartlett, University College London.

Hardware: Macintosh 8600 with Zip drive, HP scanner, and a color laser printer.

Software: Deskscan, MiniCAD and Axman.

Courtesy: Mostafa Abbaszadegan, PhD.

School of Architecture and Planning, Iran University of Science and Technology.

as the Grand Mosque, the center of social and religious activity. The thoroughfares had the highest pedestrian traffic within the city.

Second stage of the development of the city consists of development beyond the defensive wall and development of the Grand Bazaar in the south of the city. The configuration analysis of this stage of development of Yazd (figure 3), shows that the integration line simply moved to the south of the town where the new Grand Bazaar developed, so the busiest part of the city became the most integrated part of the town (red lines). After the expansion of the city beyond the defensive wall, the thoroughfares have lost their importance.

Imposition of new streets on the winding alleys and bazaar occurred in the third stage of development (figure 4). The configuration analysis of this stage of development shows that the most integrated lines in the old structure, including the Grand Bazaar and thoroughfares as the central core of the city, become less important than the new streets. These modern streets draw integration of the Old Quarter of Yazd to themselves. As a result, most activities draw from the historic part to the new part, and have caused physical and economical dilapidation of the traditional elements within the city.

The configuration analysis of the three stages of urban development of Yazd by space syntax software highlights the importance of proper interactive computer media to explore the detailed property of spaces. It also shows the capability of the software in predicting the role of each space in design stage before it actually being built.

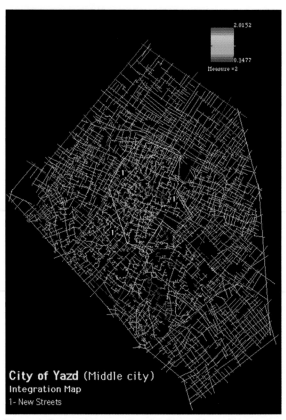

Figure 4: Integration map showing imposition of new streets

Digital Hybrids

DIGITAL HYBRIDS

Hybrids are fusion and superimposition of diverse drawing types intended to be seen as one drawing.

The fusion of two or more drawings usually results in experimental hybrid graphics with variations in scale, type of drawing, digital image manipulation technique and the use of overlapping and layering elements. Hybrids offer opportunities to explore and experiment with the presentation, to emphasize, de-emphasize, compose and de-compose specific parts of a design-drawing.

Hybrids may be divided into three basic categories:

• Fusion and superimposition of ideas
• Fusion and superimposition of media or image types
• Fusion and superimposition of techniques

Architects and designers have begun to experiment very recently with multi-media presentation techniques for architectural drawings that reach beyond the purpose of mere presentation. Such drawings often play an important role in the development of architectural ideas and new movements, and they are significantly different from drawings that merely present or document a building after it is finished or before its construction.

Digital Collage: Mixed Media

The scoreboards are depicted as messengers of the media blitz. The bottom image was generated to promote ideas of architectural design and its impact on contemporary times. It is comprised mainly of three photographs of a physical model that were scanned and collaged in Photoshop to show varying dramatic views of a scoreboard. The image is overlaid with text that takes its cue from the many activities, i.e., advertising, public address, news that the scoreboard will be used for. The image is designed to seduce, mirroring the dynamism and complexity that we, the consuming public, must decipher every day. Meteoresque tigers rocket out of an explosion of steel, as a cyborg princess, encased in technology, looks on. The graphic employs the following media: physical modeling, photography, clip-art, AutoCAD drawings, hand sketches and text.

Project: Paul Brown Stadium, Cincinnati, Ohio
Courtesy: NBBJ

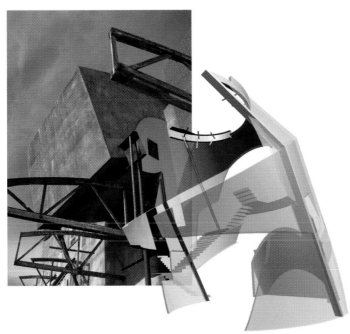

Digital Photmontage

The photomontage is digitally stitched together to unfold a space that is very difficult to photograph. This was done by photographing the space from a single vantage and then carefully rearranging and stitching the images in Photoshop.

The building recollects forward, acknowledging its past and the history of the area, while moving decisively forward to create the landmark headquarters for a digital motion picture graphic design company.

Project: Pittard Sullivan Office Building

Courtesy:
Eric Owen Moss Architects
Digital Image: Paul Groh

■ Digital Architecture

061

DIGITAL PHOTOMONTAGE
3D Model + Site Photograph

Computer generated images placed in an real context have an instant impact in testing and presenting design solutions.

Two-dimensional Autocad drawings were converted to three-dimensional meshes during the initial phase of design. As the design evolves in plan and section, the updated solution is continuously tested in three dimensions. In this case, several site photos were taken before the design process began. The site image is prepared in Photoshop and combined with images produced in 3D Studio. The final presentation includes several views created from a single model.

Hardware: Pentium 200 MHz PC.

Software: AutoCAD, 3D Studio, Lightscape, Photoshop.

Project name: 707

Credits:
Firm: AJLA
Architectural Design and Drawing: John Lumsden

DIGITAL PHOTOMONTAGE
3D Model + Site Photograph

Initial design was made using physical models which were then immediately transferred into a Microstation model of the urban context of Columbus Circle. After initial massing was set and building envelopes and zoning tested, the model was imported into Softimage for continuing development of the initial design. Variations and material and spatial relationships were more easily studied in Softimage with faster rendering engines and more advanced animation capabilities. Text, characters, and scanned images generated in Photoshop, Microstation, and Illustrator were texture-mapped onto the surfaces of the glass curtain walls.

Hardware: PC based computer

Software: Microstation, Softimage, Photoshop.

Project: Columbus Circle Tower

Courtesy:
HLW International, New York

The image showing the view to the south, and the lower lake, at a specific orientation, time of year and hour, for the wife's study. The final effect was scanning in the actual site with Photoshop, splicing into a Form•Z rendering and then transcribing to PageMaker.

Hardware: Power Macintosh G3

Software: Form•Z and Adobe Photoshop

Project: Quiet Lake
Courtesy: Bartholomew Voorsanger, Tatsuya Utsumi and Jean Luc Briquet

Velaspace **Velaspace**

Hybrid Collage:

Original sketches, photos and well-known works of art were collaged as a critical comment on the vulnerability of human occupation in Cyberspace. The images of accepted and gender specific proportional systems and a looming numerical matrix create a spatially ambiguous environment.

Hardware: PowerMac 9600/300
Software: Photoshop 4.0

Project: Way-finding in the Digital Realm
Courtesy: Barbara Ambach, Architect
College of Architecture and Planning, University of Colorado at Denver.

Hybrid Collage:

Initial design sketches and graphics from paper collages were scanned into Adobe Photoshop 3.0.5 on a Macintosh Power PC 7100/66 with 40 MB RAM. Signage and additional graphics were created in Adobe Illustrator 6.0 and imported to the digital image. A three-dimensional model was constructed in Strata StudioPro Blitz to study building massing. Texturing, layering, and line strengthening are completed in Photoshop to unify diverse pieces and capture the spirit of the final building's form and geometry.

Hardware: Macintosh Power PC 7100/66
Software: Strata StudioPro Blitz, Adobe Illustartor, Photoshop.

Project: Travel Center of America Prototype
Courtesy: van Dijk Pace Westlake Architects
Karen Skunta & Company

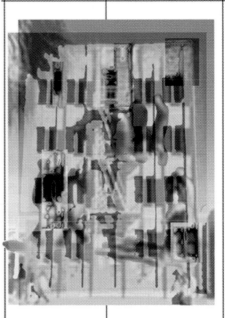

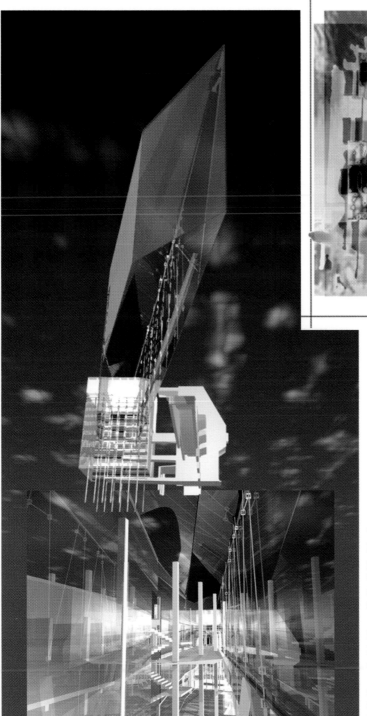

Inscriptions

A 'close read' of an existing building in Venice Beach, California. Inscriptions (photos and sketches) of people, structure and atmosphere were manipulated with various screens and filters creating a dense overlay recording the building's memory and history.

Hardware: PowerMac 9600/300
Software: Photoshop 4.0

Velaspace Prototype

Fully rendered Form•Z perspectives exported to Photoshop where they were collaged and enhanced with light effects and background filters (see page 030 for orthographic documentation).

Hardware: PowerMac 9600/300
Software: Form•Z 2.9.3, Photoshop 4.0 & QuarkXPress 3.3

Courtesy: Barbara Ambach, Architect College of Architecture and Planning, University of Colorado at Denver.

DIGITAL HYBRID
Collage in Layers

In everyday practice, architects are using photorealistic architectural images to better understand and judge design. However, there is often a need to present ideas in less defined and more artistic terms. In such a situation, architectural collage with a dose of artistic freedom is the best way to create a rendering. Images below are an example of such architectural collages. Their intention is to stimulate imagination but also not to overcommit on the design.

Image process/Technique: All studies were modeled in AutoCAD, rendered in 3D Studio, and edited in Adobe Photoshop using multiple layers and levels of transparencies. Image editing programs like Photoshop or Painter enable designer to go beyond hard line feel of computer images and give them more artistic, soft touch.

Hardware: PC based Pentium II with 3D graphic accelerator cards.

Software: AutoCAD, 3D Studio Max, Photoshop.

Projects:
Upper image: Variations of theme of Renaissance
Lower image: Brockton Medical Center
Courtesy: Andrej Zarzycki

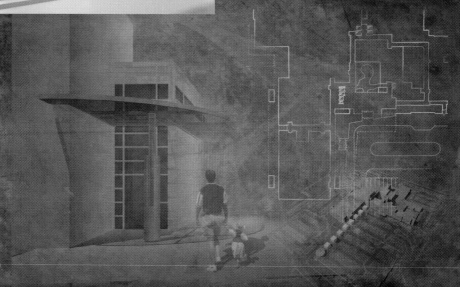

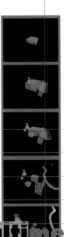

Multimedia

Multimedia

MULTIMEDIA

Multimedia simply means many or more than one medium. A variety of media such as video, sound, graphics, scanned image, text, animation, etc., when employed to construct one computer presentation, is usually called as multimedia presentation. The method of presenting in multimedia itself is hybrid in its nature. Computer slide shows, animations, digital videos are such types.

Hypermedia is another term that usually refers to multimedia that are interactive in nature or can be controlled by the user. QuickTime Virtual Reality animations and presentations created with authoring software with interactive controls fall in this type.

All multimedia formats may be divided into two basic categories: 1. Interactive Multimedia, and 2. Multimedia Authoring or Composition.

ANIMATION (non-interactive)

Representation of movement created by a series of sequential still images. The basic components and considerations of animation include:
• Keyframe (for defining object paths)
• Object path (for defining object movement)
• Object geometries (for location/form)
• Object characteristics (for defining object surfaces and materials)
• Frame rates (speed and smoothness of transition)
• Physical and gravity based models
• Waveform, flexi-objects & liquid modeling)

QUICKTIME VR (interactive) Technology is discussed in the later part of this section with its basic working priciples.

The examples shown in this section are several multimedia presentations that were created using 3D model, rendering, video capture, sound, digital video editing, and effects.

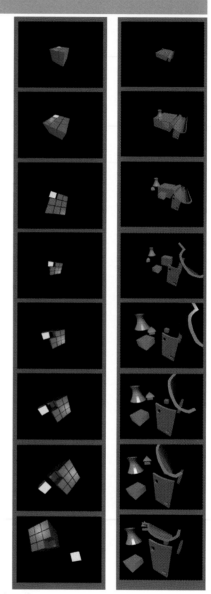

Analytic Animation

Frames taken from two QuickTime movies (with sound) that were modeled in Form•Z and rendered and animated in Infini-D in a Macintosh platform. Left image illustrates the relationship between a unit cube and a whole cube, whereas the right image separates the basic constituent components from the total mass of Le Corbusier's Parliament Building in Chandigarh, India.

Courtesy: M. Saleh Uddin

Collage Movie

These images were taken from an animated collage sequencing through a series of analytic studies of a Native American culture, the Salt River Pima Maricopa Indian Community of Arizona. The study was conducted with the cooperation of various members of the Community with the help of Arizona State University. The study was not to appear linear as most historical accounts of Native American culture tend to be, but rather simultaneously historical, projective, and documentary. The intent of the Quicktime movie was to illustrate the various disparate influences and concerns of the present Pima Maricopas within the context of an evolving people. The sequence shows pieces of historical documentation, present conditions and cultural identity, excerpts from infringing casino development, and geographic information.

The advantage of such a Quicktime movie is that one can layer audio clips, video clips, still images, and text. The use of carefully created transitions between images and sequences allows for the strategic overlap of the images resulting in a richly layered collage of information. As a Quicktime movie, the ease of playing the movie for clients and committees is a major asset, as well as the ability to transport the movie files across great distances as a cohesive whole, explaining the project without the presence of the designer.

The animation was created using Adobe Premiere, with images imported from scanned sources, Photoshop images, USGS data, and sound from Native American artists. These sources are then imported into Premiere, and placed along timelines with sequences placed between discrete image chains. Premiere then flattens the seperate timelines and audio clips into a Quicktime movie, varying from between 8 to 30 frames per second.

Hardware and Software:
PowerMacIntosh CPU's - 7100/66 with 80 MB RAM with Apple 17" monitor, 7100/80 with 40 MB RAM with Apple 17" monitor PowerMacIntosh G3 Powerbook with 32 MB RAM Connectix QuickCam Digital Camera, HP 4c scanner.

Project: Salt River Pima Maricopa Indian Community Cultural Center, Scottsdale, Arizona
Courtesy: MAZE Design Collaborative, Inc.
Animation: John and Linda Maze

Animation:

Frames (left image) from an animation sequence produced by *Arquitectonica* for an exhibition at the Cooper Hewitt National Design Museum (a branch of Smithsonian) in New York. Animation incorporates the techniques of special effects including morph through video editing to illustrate the building growing out of a comet. The city was modeled and rendered in 3D Studio Max version 2. Maps for the models were created in Photoshop. Animation was rendered in 3D Studio Max and produced on a perception board. Video clips assembled and edited in Adobe Premiere.

Project: E Walk at Times Square, New York, New York
Courtesy: Arquitectonica

The sequence of images (above) were taken from an exploratory animation that takes its cue from icons of the city of Minneapolis, in particular the city hall clock tower, and provides a sort of commentary on institutional architecture, rock stars, troubled youth and the ever present watchdog, father time. It is played out against a landscape of various architectural solutions from projects both real and ephemeral, taking the position that it is possible to be in two places at one time. The end result is a moving collage of Dali-esque imagery, deconstructing buildings and out-of-control machinery.

The computer models were constructed in AES, a modeling program designed by IBM in the mid-eighties. Most of the material maps (polygon surfaces) were scanned from clip art found in magazines, books, etc. Camera flight paths and kinematics were created in the keyframer window of 3DStudio. When each frame was completed it was deposited in a reservoir drive that was accessible to an editing station. Frames were then dragged onto a timeline and placed on SVHS tape one by one. The final edit, including a soundtrack by the design team, won first place of 356 entries in Architectural Record's computer delineation awards.

Project: Big Bang
Courtesy : LOGICERROR (Paul Q. Davis, David E. Koenen, Derek McCallum, Chris Mullen)

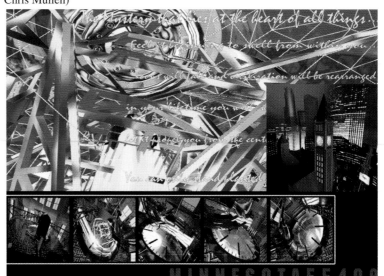

Left image: Exterior digital "fly-over" sequence. Miami International Airport Terminal
Right image: Interior retail shopping mall sequence. Miami International Airport Terminal
Courtesy: Arquitectonica

QuickTime Virtual Reality

Apple® QuickTime® VR Authoring Studio allows the creation of interactive, three-dimensional virtual worlds by offering several types of Virtual Reality construction tools and the means to integrate them into an interactive presentation. QuickTime VR (QTVR) Authoring Studio tools allow for the creation of 360° panoramas from photographs or computer models, and provide the ability to create and examine objects in the round. It is also possible to create scenes which link the multiple QTVR elements to form an interactive virtual environment. The five basic modules which make up the Authoring Studio include a Panorama Maker, Panorama Stitcher, Object Maker, Scene Maker and Project Manager. While the Authoring Studio software runs only on the Mac® OS platform, final QuickTime VR movies may be viewed in either Macintosh or Windows platforms with the proper plug-ins for web browsers or through the use of applications which can play QuickTime movies.

Image courtesy:
Apple® web site

QuickTime panoramic movies are constructed by tiling or dividing a panoramic image into a number of frames which are then joined together as if mapped to the interior of an imaginary sphere. The resulting space or image which is presented to the person viewing the QTVR node is the vantage point of a person standing in the center of the virtual sphere looking outward. The construction of a QTVR object movie follows a similar principle: an object is placed in the center of the imaginary sphere as the viewer rotates around the perimeter. A QTVR scene is constructed

through the integration of QTVR panoramic and object movies by placing and linking representative "nodes" of the movies in a plan view or map of the project in the Scene Maker window. The linking of nodes and creation of "hot spots" determine the form of the interactive QTVR movie.

QTVR: Conceptual Revelations

Typically, many QTVR images found on the Web are "objective" representations of the world around us: vacation vistas, college campus tours and objects of commerce and desire. At Ohio State, a graduate-level seminar is offered which explores the critical and creative potential of QTVR to represent architectural space. In the student project which follows (illustrations 1-5), QTVR is utilized to allow the viewer to pass seamlessly from within a digital (virtual) model to the physical (real) realm of an architectural project, while revealing critical design concepts. The construction of a non-linear narrative and the use of interactive hot-spots and links help to establish the critical stance of the architectural project.

In the project, a temporary kiosk disseminates information to students on the campus of the University, exposing political relationships which exist in the University. The kiosk propagates information through the combination of a video broadcast and the use of framed views within the structure to specific University buildings. Through the use of QTVR hot spots and links, the student was able to communicate the intentions of the project. In the QTVR movie, a video monitor acts as a link (figure 5) which reveals the project's political agenda: By clicking on the video monitor with a mouse, the user is confronted with two contrasting images of the University: University as educational center and University as business. Through the superimposition of specific panoramas and views, the viewer experiences a series of montaged spaces to discover a new architectural space between the University's facade and body.

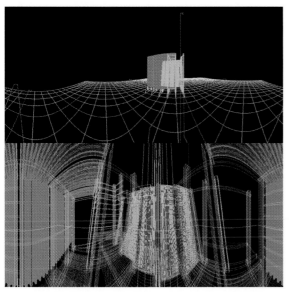

figure 1
form-Z generated panoramic images.
In form-Z, the viewer is placed in the center of a scene, then a panoramic image is rendered and saved as a PICT file. This PICT image is imported to the QTVR Panorama Maker to generate a QTVR panoramic movie. (Renderings by Javier Pagán)

figure 2
QTVR Panorama Stitcher.
A series of photographic images taken with a QTVR tripod head are converted to PICT files, then added to the QTVR Panorama Stitcher to generate a QTVR panoramic movie.
Dialog box from QuickTime® VR Authoring Studio, © Apple®

figure 3
QTVR panoramic PICT images generated with the Panorama Stitcher.
The PICT images are tiled by the Panorama Stitcher to form QTVR panoramic movies.
(Panoramic images by Javier Pagán)

073

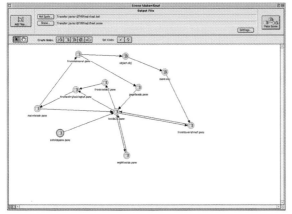

figure 4
QTVR Scene Maker.
Construction of the final QTVR Scene in the QTVR Scene Maker window by the linking of source material node icons: objects, panoramas and links to the world wide web. Links between nodes appear as arrowed lines depicting the interactive navigation of the final QTVR movie.
Dialog box from QuickTime® VR Authoring Studio, © Apple®

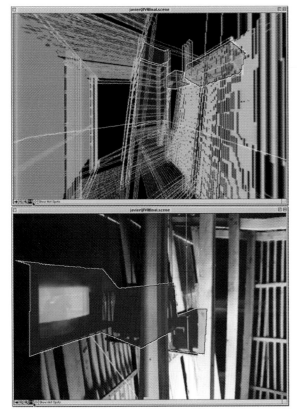

figure 5
QTVR hot spots.
Hot spots mark the placement of interactive links within the nodes of the QTVR Scene. When viewing the final QTVR movie, the user has the ability to "Show Hot Spots" to assist navigation through the virtual space.
(Screen captures from Apple® QuickTime® Movie

Hardware used:
Kaidan Quick Pan QP-5 and Quick Pan Magnum QPX-2 tripod heads.
Olympus D-500L digital camera.
PowerComputing PowerCenter Pro 210, 128 MB RAM.
Iomega Zip and Jaz drives.

Software used:
Apple® QuickTime® VR Authoring Studio, auto-des-sys form•Z, Adobe Photoshop.

Getting started: What you'll need to create QTVR panoramas, objects and scenes.

Apple® QuickTime® VR Authoring Studio software from Apple: http://www.apple.com/.

Apple recommended minimum system configuration for using QuickTime VR Authoring Studio includes: Mac OS-based computer with a PowerPC processor, 16 MB RAM for the application, 40 MB RAM hard disk space, and a CD-ROM drive.

Requirements for playing QTVR media include: QuickTime extension version 2.5 or later, QuickTime VR extension version 2.0.1 or later, MoviePlayer version 2.5 or later, or SimpleText

To photograph images for the construction of QTVR Panoramas, either a manual SLR, digital or video camera is acceptable. If available, a digital camera saves both time and cost to the project. A QuickTime VR Tripod Head is necessary to create photographic QuickTime VR Panoramas; QTVR tripod heads rotate 360° to capture a sequence of photos which will be stitched together to form the QTVR panorama. QTVR tripod heads may be purchased from a number of manufacturers including Kaidan: http://www.kaidan.com/. QuickTime VR Object Rigs are also available for purchase: rotating platforms used to photograph objects for the creation of QuickTime VR Objects.

Other software applications may be used in conjunction with QTVR Authoring Studio, such as auto-des-sys form•Z 3-D modeling software and Adobe Photoshop for image editing. A camera and QTVR tripod head are not necessary to construct QTVR modules when working with computer generated imagery.

All images on pages 73 and 74 are Courtesy of Lisa Tilder, The Ohio State University.

(Text for QTVR section is authored by Lisa Tilder, Assistant Professor, Ohio State University. Illustrations have been taken from a QTVR project produced at Ohio State University by Javier Pagán.)

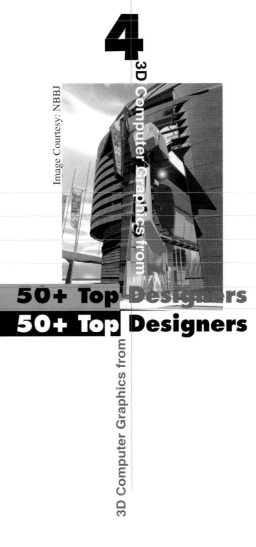

4

3D

3D Computer Graphics from

Image Courtesy: NBBJ

50+ Top Designers

50+ Top Designers

3D Computer Graphics from

Image: Eric Owen Moss Architects

DIGITAL ARCHITECTURE
3D Computer Graphics from 50 Top Designers

Advanced Media Design
(for Kohn Pedersen Fox, Robert A. M. Stern Architects)
Anthony Ames Architect
Natalye Appel Architects
Architecture Research Office
Arquitectonica
R.L. Binder, FAIA
Centerbrook Architects
Office dA
Davis Carter Scott
Deiss and Associates with Oliver + Ray Architects
Delphi Productions
Peter Edgeley
Einhorn Yaffee Prescott
Ellerbe Becket
Felderman + Keatinge Associates
Form:uLA
Fox & Fowle Architects
Carl Hampson
HDR Architecture
HLW International
HNTB
House + House Architects
Inglese Architecture
Helmut Jahn of Murphy/Jahn
The Jerde Partnership International

Kajima Corporation
Kiss + Cathcart Architects
KovertHawkins Architects
John Lumsden
Machado and Silvetti Associates
Morphosis
Eric Owen Moss Architects
NBBJ
Nelson Design
Cesar Pelli & Associates
Pentagram Architecture
Perkins & Will
Polshek and Partners Architects
Richard Rauh & Associates
Resolution: 4 Architecture
Rogers Marvel Architects
Schwartz Architects
TRO/The Ritchie Organization
Tsao & McKown Architects
Bernard Tschumi Architects
van Dijk Pace Westlake Architects
Venturi, Scott Brown and Associates
Vistaara Architects
Voorsanger & Associates Architetcs
Wendy Evans Joseph Architects
Ken Yeang

Advanced Media Design for
Kohn Pedersen Fox, Robert A. M. Stern Architects

Web Site: www.amdrendering.com

Providence, Rhode Island 02903

Kohn Pedersen Fox • The Esplanade Mall, Suntec City, Singapore
Robert A. M. Stern Architetcs • Proposed Tower Interior, Trading Floor

Profile:

The office of Advanced Media Design, Inc. (AMD) was founded in 1992 when the two principals Richard Dubrow and Jon Kletzien graduated with architecture degrees from the Rhode Island School of Design, subsequently two more RISD graduates joined the office, in 1995, James Kuhn, and in 1998, Julien Roche. The firm was founded as a digital illustration studio specifically for architects. In 1997 the office was the first to claim the prestigious Hugh Ferriss Memorial Prize using a digital piece, with their depiction of Friedrich St. Florian's winning entry in the National WWII Memorial competition. The Ferriss prize, which is awarded to the outstanding architectural illustration of the year by the American Society of Architectural Perspectivists, is the premiere award for architectural illustrators in North America.

AMD's Use of Digital Media:

The only media in the office is digital, both three-dimensional modeling and painting are done on the machines. "Our concentration has always been on studying other illustrators, leaving technology questions for our indispensable outside consultants. We almost always buy machines that are a generation behind, try to get the most out of the machinery and software at hand, and stick with proven operating systems. Work is presently done on various Pentium 133 and Pentium Pro 200 computers with 64 to 128 megs of RAM running Windows NT 4.0 and 95, digitizing tablets, as well as a color printer. The images included were all done using AutoCAD (r12-14) for modeling, 3Dstudio (r 4.0), 3DS Max (r1.2) or 3DS VIZ (r.2) for rendering, Ron Scotts Hi-Res QFX (r4-6) for texture maps and final image painting, and Photoshop (r 3-4) for image sizing and format conversion.

The Esplanade Mall, Suntec City, Singapore

Kohn Pedersen Fox
The Esplanade Mall, Suntec City, Singapore

Drawing Process / Image Technique:

The illustration was to show the proposed mall/office building and its relationship to the existing park.

Hardware and Software:

Hardware: Micron Millennia Pro2, Microtek ScanMaker3, Wacom Tablet, Fargo Pictura 3000.
Software: AutoCAD r.12 for DOS, 3D Studio r. 4 for DOS, Hi Rez Q/FX r.4 for DOS, Photoshop r.2.5 for Windows.

Credits:

Architect/Designer: Kohn Pedersen Fox Associates
Partner in Charge-Bill Pedersen, FAIA
Digital Image: Advanced Media Design
3D Modeling: Jon Kletzien, James Kuhn
Rendering: Richard Dubrow, Jon Kletzien
Post Production: Richard Dubrow, Jon Kletzien, James Kuhn

Robert A. M. Stern Architects
Proposed Tower Interior, Trading Floor

Drawing Process / Image Technique:

The illustration was used to show the trading rooms major design feature, the skylight, the reflection of the existing surrounding buildings in tower body (to right) and the activity on the trading floor.

Hardware and Software:

Hardware: Micron Millennia Pro2, Gateway GP6-333, Microtek ScanMaker3, Wacom Tablet, Fargo Pictura 3000.
Software: AutoCAD r.13, 3D Studio MAXr1.2, Hi Rez Q/FX r.6, Photoshop r.4.

Credits:

Architect/Designer: Robert A. M. Stern Architects
Partner in Charge: Graham S. Wyatt
3D Modeling: James Kuhn, Julien Roche
Rendering: Richard Dubrow, James Kuhn
Post Production: Jon Kletzien, Richard Dubrow, James Kuhn

Anthony Ames Architect

Atlanta, Georgia 30308

House in Scaly Mountain

Profile:

Anthony Ames received his architectural education from Harvard University and Georgia Tech and is a fellow of the American Academy of Rome. His work has received design awards from *Progressive Architecture* magazine, *Architectural Record* magazine and the American Institute of Architects. He has taught architecture at Columbia University, the Rhode Island School of Design, Harvard University, Princeton University, Georgia Tech, the University of Virginia and other places. He currently maintains an office in Atlanta, Georgia but his projects tend to be elsewhere.

Hardware and Software:

Macintosh PowerMac. Form•Z and Adobe Photoshop.

Digital Drawing Technique / Process:

The images were hand drawn in ink on vellum from computer generated three point perspectives. The line drawings were then scanned back into the computer and digitally colorized.

080

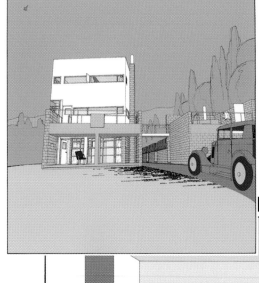

Concept:

The site was cut into the western slope of a mountain with access via a private road from below. The most desirable view is toward the south southwest. The mountain side site has been "worked over" and formalized in hopes of encouraging an interaction with the mountain by providing a variety of spatial experiences working vertically and horizontally and a variety of ways to access these spaces. This "promenade architectural" and formalization of the site attempts to accommodate various requirements of the program - a small garden, a lawn, space for vehicles, a terrace with a fireplace/barbecue, a belvedere, storage, and various other amenities.

Credits:

Architect: Anthony Ames
Assistant: Clark Tefft
Computer: Alan Brown

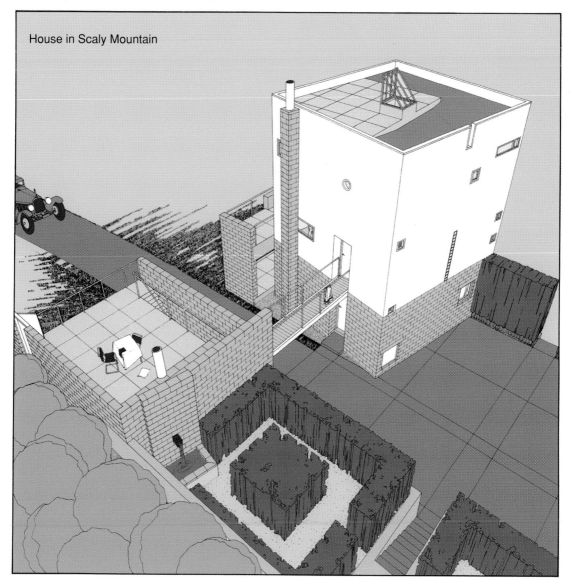

House in Scaly Mountain

Natalye Appel Architects

E-mail: Appelarchs@aol.com
Houston, Texas 77019

Lowe/Booker Studio

Profile:

Natalye Appel Architects is a six person firm specializing in a creative, collaborative approach to design as an expression of the clients' needs, the site and the methods and materials of construction. Our devotion to design clarity and appropriateness has earned us numerous awards and wide publication of our work, much of which has been accomplished within very modest construction budgets.

Natalye Appel's Use of Digital Media:

MiniCAD has become the primary tool for 2-dimensional drafting during the Design Development and Construction Document phases. In D.D., design options can be explored quickly, enabling a flexible design relationship with clients. In C.D.'s, databases are used within MiniCAD to formulate window, door and finish schedules, simplifying coordination. 3-D modeling is used as a design tool for exploring multiple options and a presentation technique to aid in visualizing spatial relationships.

Hardware:

Apple Power Macintosh 7100/80, 7200/75, G3/233 DT, Power Book 1400cs, Power Computing PowerBase 180.

Software:

DiehlGraphsoft MiniCAD 7, Lightworks Superlite Renderer Plug-in, Adobe Photoshop 3.0.

Digital Drawing Technique / Process:

Models are both built and rendered with DiehlGraphsoft MiniCAD using Lightworks SuperLite Quickdraw 3D plug-in. Images were cropped and sized with Adobe Photoshop.

Concept:

Lowe/Booker Studio
The sawtooth roof forms of this sculpture/jewelry studio and guest house both evoke the industrial forms of its surrounding neighborhood and capture the soft northern light its client prefers. In plan, the L-shape creates a natural court around an existing pecan tree.

Credits:

Natalye Appel, AIA, Lonnie Hoogeboom, Donna Kacmar, AIA, Rosanne Ramos, Shannon Sasser, Stuart Smith

Architecture Research Office

Web Site: www.aro.net
E-mail: aro@aro.net

New York, New York 10014

Sunshine Mesa House, Telluride, Colorado

Profile:

Architecture Research Office was established 1993 and is currently a fourteen person firm. ARO has designed a wide variety of projects including architecture, interiors and exhibitions. The starting point of each project is its physical, social and economic conditions. Every undertaking becomes a process of inquiry: research and analysis frame experiments in material and construction. Drawings, models, study and reflection are the tools for shaping each design.

ARO's Use of Digital Media:

Computers are an integral design tool in the office. Mini-CAD and Form•Z as well as cardboard are used to study potential schemes. As the project develops the computer models become more precise; construction details and views are checked in 3D. The speed with which the models give feedback on the design determines their worth. Throughout, perspectives are generated to develop an intuition for the project and used with collage to create drawings for the client.

Hardware:

Power computing Power Centre Pro 210 MHz / 136 MB RAM, Mac OS 7.6.1.

Software:

Form•Z Renderzone 9.5.5, Adobe Photoshop 5.0, MiniCAD 7.1.

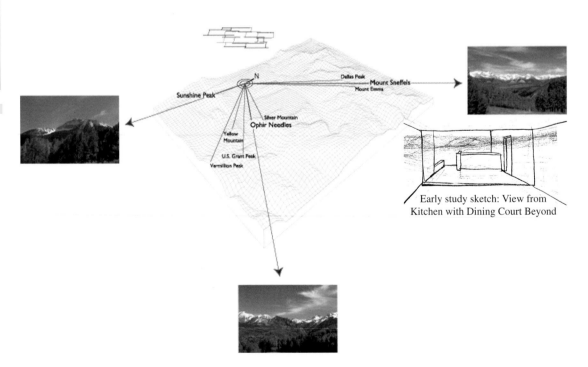

Early study sketch: View from
Kitchen with Dining Court Beyond

Drawing Process / Image Technique:

An initial design was generated using MiniCAD and cardboard sketch models. The importance of particular views from the house required the accurate modeling of a 13 x 17 mile area (as far as the eye can see) in Form•Z. Using this model and Minicad, the relationship between long distance and near views specific to each room was studied in 3-D; window and mullion sizes and locations were subtly adjusted. Construction details affecting the appearance of the house in the landscape were tested.

Design Concept:

Located atop a mesa in Colorado, a series of concrete and Cor-ten shingle walls step down a knoll and orient the home to specific spectacular views of surrounding mountains. Two ranges are seen along the axis of the walls and on the perpendicular axis. Thus the plan is understood from inside looking out and interlocking interior and exterior spaces are established, woven to minimize the apparent size of the home in the landscape.

Credits:

Staff: Stephen Cassell, partner-in-charge; John Quale, project architect; Adam Yarinsky, Scott Abrahams, Mikael Hoilund, Jiayur Hsu, Josh Pulver, Monica Rivera, Martha Skinner, Kim Yao.

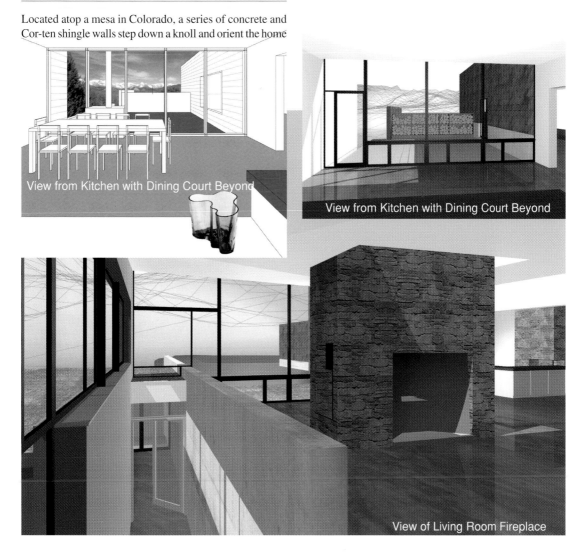

View from Kitchen with Dining Court Beyond

View from Kitchen with Dining Court Beyond

View of Living Room Fireplace

085

Arquitectonica

Web Site: www.arquitectonica.com

Miami, Florida 33131

American Airlines-Miami Heat Arena, Miami, Florida
Miami International Airport, Miami, Florida
Miranova, Columbus, Ohio

▌ Profile:

Arquitectonica is based in Miami, with offices in New York, Los Angeles, Paris, Manila, Lima, Hong Kong and Shanghai. Since its founding in 1977, Arquitectonica has developed an international practice recognized for excellence and innovation. The firm is best known for its creative ability to design with memorable imagery and regional identity.

With a professional staff of over 130, Arquitectonica is a full-service firm, with all aspects of a project, from initial planning to final drawings, accomplished totally in-house. The practice is firmly committed to CADD design and production. Currently in use is AutoCad in the production of working drawings and final documents.

Arquitectonica's designs have won numerous American Institute of Architects and Progressive Architecture design awards. The firm is widely published in national and international publications such as *Time, Newsweek, Life, Fortune,* and *Business Week,* as well as numerous professional journals such as *Architectural Record, Progressive Architecture, Architectural Design* (England), *Domus* (Italy), *Global Architecture* (Japan), *L'Architecture D'aujourd'hui* (France) and *Häuser* (Germany). Arquitectonica's designs have been exhibited in major museums and institutions in the United States, Europe, Latin America, and Asia including shows in Paris, Buenos Aires, Rome, Frankfurt, Rotterdam, Bordeaux, Brussels, Zurich, Tokyo, New York, San Francisco, San Diego, Minneapolis, Chicago, Houston, Boston and Philadelphia.

▌ Arquitectonica's Use of digital media:

Arquitectonica primarily uses digital imaging to assist the client in visualizing the project during design development. Digital animation sequences in videos have been used to win public support for a project, to sell condominium units and luxury sports suites, and for display in an exhibition on Arquitectonica at the Smithsonian.

Atlanta Arena /CNN Center, Atlanta, Georgia

American Airlines-Miami Heat Arena

Hardware:

Dual Pentium II 300 and 400 MHz processors, 256 MB RAM, Matrox and Oxygen video cards, DPS Perception PVR non-linear editing board, HP 2500 Plotter.

Software:

3D Studio Max version 2; Photoshop version 4.

Digital Drawing Technique / Process:

The images were modeled and rendered in 3D Studio Max version 2 and finished in Photoshop version 4. 3D models were used throughout design development to facilitate client visualization; the client used the images to sell the project as well as the arena's naming rights.

Concept:

This 19,500-seat indoor arena is designed primarily for basketball, but is adaptable for cultural and music events. It is part of a larger mixed-use development which includes entertainment, restaurants, retail and office space. The mission of the arena project is to provide a state of-the-art facility and surrounding urban district that stand out as a grand civic landmark. A pure ellipse is formed by a girded structural frame to create the core of this multipurpose arena. A series of "sails" or "prows" are suspended from this frame swirling in one direction. They conceal mechanical and functional components, yet reveal at intervals the concrete and glass ellipse and the activities within the building.

American Airlines-Miami Heat Arena, Miami, Florida

Credits:

Design Principals:
Bernardo Fort-Brescia, FAIA
Laurinda Hope Spear, FAIA

3D Computer Graphics:
Eric M. Blumberg, Lizette
Quimper, Damion Cera and
Damian Ponton

Miami International Airport, Miami, Florida

Hardware:

Dual Pentium II 300 and 400 MHz processors, 256 MB RAM, Matrox and Oxygen video cards, DPS Perception PVR non-linear editing board, HP 2500 Plotter.

Software:

3D Studio Max version 4, 3D Studio Max version 2 and Perception Video Board.

Digital Drawing Technique / Process:

The image was modeled and rendered in 3D Studio Max version 2, finished in Photoshop version 4. The study model was used to aid in the design of the roof and in the coordination of the plans and elevations. It has also helped the client to visualize the project and to present the project to the general public.

Concept:

Three vault sizes following structural modules are mixed randomly to create the rippled effect of waves or clouds over the new Miami International Airport main terminal. The terminal's wavy roof surface is terraced to allow for clerestory light into the international arrivals / immigration hall, duty-free shopping mall and customs areas. The green glass edge responds to the site boundary that allows for aircraft positions and rotation. A hotel/office slab placed behind the terminal has a simple rectangular form that tapers in reverse reflecting the white curving forms of the terminal roof.

Credits:

Design Principals: Bernardo Fort-Brescia, FAIA
Laurinda Hope Spear, FAIA
3D Computer Graphics: Eric Blumberg, Lizette Quimper, Damion Cera and Damian Ponton.

Miami International Airport, Miami, Florida

Miranova, Columbus, Ohio

▌ Hardware:

Dual Pentium II 300 and 400 MHz processors, 256 MB RAM, Matrox and Oxygen video cards, DPS Perception PVR non-linear editing board, HP 2500 Plotter.

▌ Software:

3D Studio Max 2; Photoshop version 4; LightScape version 3.0 for interiors.

▌ Digital Drawing Technique / Process:

This image was modeled and rendered in 3D Studio Max version 2 and finished in Photoshop version 4. The lighting was done in LightScape. Modeling was used throughout design process to facilitate client visualization. The client then commissioned ARQ to produce final images to sell the project.

▌ Concept:

Miranova is a mixed-use "community within a city" to be built on a six-acre site on the Sciotto riverfront south of downtown. The north facade is a sweeping curve allowing dramatic views of downtown Columbus. The complex features a 27-story, 166-unit residential luxury condominium tower with an enclosed 237-car parking garage, two office buildings to be built in phases, a freestanding commercial building and an outdoor pool and tennis court for resident use.

▌ Credits:

Design Principals: Bernardo Fort-Brescia, FAIA
Laurinda Hope Spear, FAIA
3D Computer Graphics: Eric M. Blumberg, Lizette Quimper, Damion Cera, Damian Ponton and Patricia Freedman.

Miranova, Columbus, Ohio

R. L. Binder, F.A.I.A., Architecture & Planning

E-mail: RLBFAIA@aol.com

Playa del Rey, California 90293

Hesperia Fire Station #5, Hesperia, California

Profile:

R. L. Binder, FAIA Architecture & Planning, established in 1979, is a woman-owned architecture firm providing comprehensive planning, programming, and design services. The firm has been widely published and exhibited, and is recognized nationally and internationally as a leading design firm in Southern California. RLB has created a body of architectural work that is the culmination of focused and informed creative thought. The firm's completed works include large scale institutional, commercial, and residential projects. Program functions for these projects include multi-media facilities, office/administration space, retail spaces, housing, community facilities, dining facilities, art facilities, classrooms, gallery and performance spaces, conference facilities, and recreational facilities. The firm has won numerous awards for creative and responsive design.

Use of Digital Media:

RLB utilizes the following digital media in place of traditional media: CADD with 3D modeling and rendering, scanned images, internet e-mail and web browsing for research, correspondence and access to client intranets, MS Powerpoint computer presentations, project management software using a MS Access customized relational database, and digital fax transmit and receive technology.

Hardware:

11 computer stations with Intel Pentium, Cyrix and AMD processors. Additional computer hardware equipment includes: 2 modems; 30 bit graphic scanner; facsimile scanner; digitizers; plotter; 1440 dpi four color printer; and 2 laser printers.

090

Software:

CADD: AUTOCAD r.14 with AEC Professional Suite.
Graphics: Adobe Photoshop 4.0.1, Micrografx Picture Publisher 7.0, Coreldraw, Micrografx Simply 3D, color management calibration software.
Office Software: MS Word, MS Access, MS Excel, MS Powerpoint, MS Project 98, Lantastic networking with Modemshare, and Quickbooks.
Internet Software: AOL 4.0, Internet Explorer.

Drawing Process / Digital Technique:

CADD drawings and 3-dimensional renderings are integrated with RLB's design process from programming and planning through conceptual design, design development and construction documents. Scanned images and CADD renderings/drawings are manipulated using Photoshop, Picture Publisher and Coreldraw for use in presentations, company promotional graphics, and computer based presentations.

Design Concept:

The fire station provides essential services to the community including paramedic headquarters and communications center. It is a design which welcomes the public while creating a private living area for the fire fighters. The site development includes hose drying layout area and above grade fuel tanks, as well as public and facility parking. The design creates a legible municipal facility. The operative firehouse image of a hose drying tower is not part of this project due to the program requirement of horizontal drying racks. Therefore, the station is conceived as a "western fort" in its distinct horizontally. This is accentuated by its strong horizontal bands of textured block. The entry design is a response to strong winds and weather.

Credits:

Design: Rebecca L. Binder, FAIA, and Kim A. Walsh, AIA
Digital Drawing: Chilin Huang, Architect

091

Centerbrook Architects

E-mail: last name@centerbrook.com
Web Site: www.centerbrook.com

Essex, Connecticut 06426

New Learning Resource Center, Manchester Community Technical College, Manchester, Connecticut

▋ Profile:

Centerbrook is a Limited Liability Company with 32 years experience in Architecture and Planning throughout the United States. Located in a renovated factory on the Falls River in the rural town of Essex, Connecticut, it has five partners and an overall staff of 68. The firm's approach is distinctly American–its work is eclectic and its methods democratic. Centerbrook has also developed unique interactive techniques to involve a whole population in the design of their campus or city. Centerbrook's project experience encompasses a variety of educational and institutional work, as well as several museums, churches, hotels, libraries, theaters, retail complexes, community centers, and industrial plants. The office enjoys many smaller projects as well, with over ten residences in design or construction.

▋ Use of Digital Media:

Centerbrook has employed computer-aided design (CAD) since 1982. "Our current configuration includes a Local Area Network of 60+ DOS/Windows based computers with intercommunication between computer operating systems. In addition to AutoCAD's ability to produce construction documents, Centerbrook uses AutoCAD Release 14's capabilities and AccuRender software applications to model, render, and animate building designs for presentations, multi-media productions, and high-resolution still images. This allows us to examine realistic variations of site plans and building design. Most importantly, the 3-D provides us with stunning presentation renderings and animated videos for fund-raising."

Hardware:

400 MHz dual processor Pentium II, with 512MB RAM, 100MB Zip drive, video card, UMAX scanner, HP LaserJet printer, HP color plotter.

Software:

AutoCAD Release 14, AccuRender 3.0, and Photoshop 4.0.

Drawing Process / Image Technique:

A wireframe model was created in AutoCAD Release 14 and the model was rendered with AccuRender 2.0. People were added and final image editing was completed with Photoshop 4.0. Additional animations were created using AccuRender 3.0.

Design Concept:

The placement of the new facility at Manchester Community Technical College creates a new oval courtyard within the heart of campus. Vertical structures around the courtyard act as landmarks, with a glassy bridge connecting the new Learning Resource Center with the existing Lowe Building. The shiny glass and modernistic details of the oval gallery express MCTC's commitment to progressive, high-tech education in support of Connecticut's technology-based future.

Credits:

Partner-in-Charge: Chad Floyd, FAIA
Project Manager: James R. Martin, AIA
Design Team: Greg Nucci, AIA, Rich Terrell, AIA
Rendering: Padraic H. Ryan

Office dA

Boston, MA 02118

E-mail: da@officeda.com
Web Site: www.gsd.harvard.edu/info/directory/faculty/poncedeleon
Web Site: www.gsd.harvard.edu/info/directory/faculty/tehrani

"Fabricating Coincidences"
Fabrications: The Tectonic Garden, Museum of Modern Art

Profile:

Office dA is a Boston-based firm whose principal partners include Monica Ponce de Leon and Nader Tehrani.

The work of Office dA is diverse in scope and scale, ranging from the design of interiors to the broader scale of urban design and infrastructure. Among other projects, various notable designs include: Miami - Public Infrastructure for the Tropics, a project that received first prize in the 1993 Boston Society of Architects Unbuilt Architecture Competition and is published in The New City Journal of Architecture printed by Princeton Architectural Press; The Mill Road House, Casa La Roca, and The Weston House have all won first Awards in the Progressive Architecture Awards Competition, respectively in 1995,1996, and 1998; the Greene House, built in 1990, is published in Casas Internacionales and The New American House by The Whitney Library of Design; the Northeastern University Inter-faith Hall of Prayer, consisting of the redesign of a religious interior, has also been awarded a BSA Unbuilt Architecture Award and was completed in 1998. Monica Ponce de Leon and Nader Tehrani have also been awarded the 1997 Young Architects Award from the Architecture League of New York, and have been nominated for the prestigious Chrysler Award.

Office dA's Use of Digital Media:

The use of digital media has played a significant role in the projects of Office dA. Research strategies at the office however, are emphatically eclectic, and thus, the computer plays only one role among an array of representational modes that are investigated— some normative and some less conventional. In the range of media, computation has made possible certain operations that would otherwise be inconceivable; most importantly, it has permitted an unquestionable fluidity between the process of conceiving, drawing, and manufacturing that is virtually unprecedented. Also, various techniques of representation have come hand in hand with the medium -- animations, lighting techniques, and rendering programs — that are all central to our strategies of investigation. Thus, the resultant architecture can be said to have a direct relationship with its enabling medium.

For the "Fabrications" project at the Museum of Modern Art, Office dA worked closely with Milgo Bufkin to produce a folded steel plate structure using a technology that had never been attempted at that scale or with that level of complexity. Ponce de Leon and Tehrani visited the Milgo Bufkin workshop in Brooklyn and studied the potentials and limitations of their computation capabilities, laser-cutting technologies (metal cutting laser), perforation machines (numerically controlled punch), and bending processes. While the project was initially drafted "by hand", its development towards fabrication -- as coordinated by Matt LaRue — capitalized on the Milgo Bufkin's use of the computer and its connection to the manufacturing process.

Specifically, digital computation made possible three basic processes that became central the "Fabrications" project:

The perforation process involved a "punching" machine that was able to customize the density and acceleration of perforations along the surface of the steel. In that way, the steel surface was able to metamorphose from a heavy and solid base to a transparent gauze at the top. So too, the actual shape of the perforations were also customized and introduced as a template.

The outline of each steel piece (5'-0" X 10'-0") was finely laser-cut, minimizing the usual tolerance required in a construction process. In fact, over the forty-five foot length of the structure, there was no more than 1/4" to 1/2" of misalignment, and that was more due to distortions introduced by the welding procedure.

Laser-cutting was also used to produce scores in the steel surface —called "stitching" — as a way of permitting the folding process. Instead of bending plates of steel or welding different pieces of steel together, —which would result in far less precision or a larger radius on each bend— the sheets of steel are scored by laser in an offset pattern and then folded, resulting in a continuous twisted seam at the ridge of each plate — producing the illusion of a stitch between two pieces of fabric.

Hardware:

All drawings were done on Pentium Pro 200PC fit with w/ 64MB RAM and 4MB number 9 video card for speedy

094

rendering and animation processing. Additionally, for output, used 25W Laser cutter for mock-ups/models and perforation test pattern cuts. Color presentation images printed on Epson Stylus Photo 700. Silicon Graphics 02 was used for the animations.

For CAD, primarily used Microstation 95, which excels at surface modeling capabilities. AutoCAD R14 was used for specific tasks, such as align tool features. Rendering was done with Microsation's Masterpiece Package, enabling raytrace and texture mapped images. Photoshop was used for editing images. For the animations, Form•Z, 3D Studio Max, Adobe Photoshop, Macromedia Cooledit 97, and Adobe Premiere 4.2 were used.

▌ Software:

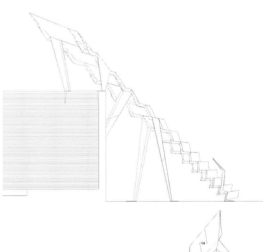

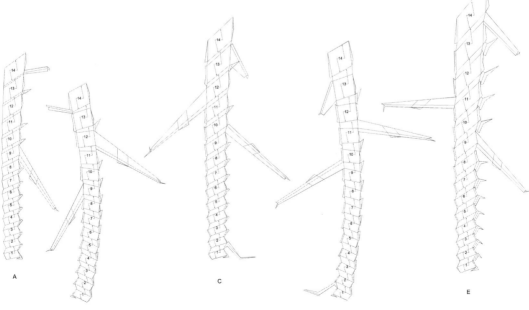

A

B

C

D

E

Drawing Process/Digital Technique:

For this project, a single 3-D model was used to develop the design (produce models, make orthogonal line drawings, create rendered images) as well as produce the finished components of the final piece through computer aided manufacturing. The surfaces of the model were flipped down to 2-D surfaces to form the true shapes. The shapes could then be cut out, perforated, and then bent along laser-scored edges.

Design Concept:

Ostensibly pertaining to the act of making, building, and manufacturing, fabrication is also connected to fabric and weaving, to notions of deceit, forgery, and fiction. It is with these complex and sometimes divergent references that Ponce de Leon and Tehrani approach "fabrication," the theme of the MoMA exhibition and the central preoccupation of their work, in general. Their installation is accordingly ambiguous; it works with folded steel plate technology as a way of blurring the traditional distinctions between structure and skin, supporting and supported building elements. Triangulation gives the steel skin rigidity, while folded columnar plates give the structure lateral bracing. This geometry is also developed on optical and anamorphic principles, yielding particular spatial readings from different points of view. The form of the installation and its relationship with the Museum wall are furthermore designed to suggest different uses and modes of inhabitation, above and below the steel plate: stair; canopy, bleacher, shelter -- not to mention sculpture, and even painting. The structure accommodates for material, spatial and programmatic variations in continuous and seamless adaptations, underplaying the normative tectonic articulation of difference. For instance, variations in the density of the perforations lighten the steel structure as it unfolds upward, allowing the gradual passage of light to the space beneath. While steel construction is customarily predicated on a trabeated system of W-sections, angles, and I-beams, this installation devises an alternative system where steel is stretched and stitched like fabric. Warps, creases and folds in a continuous structural surface substitute here for the traditional beam and column and effectively accommodate for different load and support conditions

The consistent aim was to avoid fabrication from an assembly of discreet constituent parts and devise a tectonic of seamlessness: a system that can absorb and deploy a heterogeneous set of informants and effects. It is thought

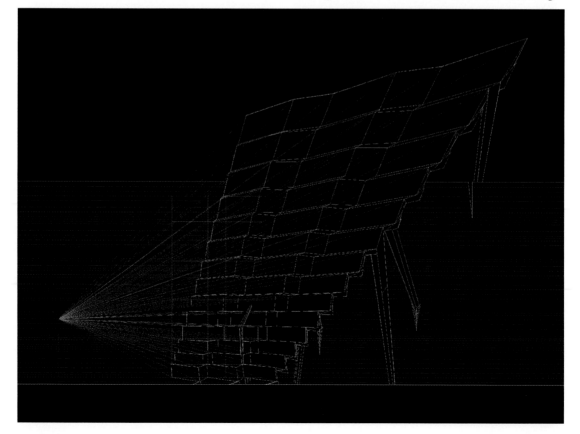

of as "fabricating coincidences," a process where issues of structure, program, lighting, and cladding are coordinated and reconciled in a continuous, homogeneous but differentiated surface.

Credits:

Design Principals: Monica Ponce de Leon, Nader Tehrani
Project Coordinator: Matt LaRue

Animation: Tim Dumbleton
Design Team: Jay Berman, Richard Lee , Jill Porter , Christian Schaller, Phillip Smith, Lee Su, Achille Rossini, Joel Schmidt

Structural Engineer: Michael J. Theiss, P.E.,
The Office of James Ruderman LLP,
Metalwork: Milgo Bufkin
President: Bruce Gitlin   Project Manager: Alex Kveton
Photography: Dan Bibb

Davis, Carter, Scott

E-mail: info@dcsdesign.com
Web Site: www.dcsdesign.com
McLean, Virginia 22102

Project: 1600 International Drive, McLean, Virginia

Profile:

Davis, Carter, Scott Ltd, with offices in McLean, Virginia and Washington, D.C., provides quality planning, architectural and interior architectural design services for corporate, high technology, hospitality, governmental, educational, and health care facilities. The firm has received over 50 international, national and local design awards, including the Interior Architecture Firm of the Year for 1994 by the Metropolitan Washington Chapter of the Associated Builders and Contractors.

Use of Digital Media:

The digital medium allows the design team to explore and present design ideas using both traditional and cutting-edge techniques. The designer and digital designer/artist participate in an interactive process to transform traditional hand sketches into an interactive walk-through. The de-sign is enhanced through further definition and clarification. Digital media improves the communication of design ideas both within the firm design team as well as between the architect and client.

Hardware:

Pentium Pro 200 w/ 128 MB of RAM, Matrox Millenium Graphics Card w/ 4MB of RAM. Pentium II 300 w/256 MB of RAM, Matrox Millenium Graphics Card w/ 8 MB of RAM. HP ScanJet 4c

Software:

AutoCAD r12 & r13, Accurender versions 2 & 3(beta), Adobe Photoshop 3.0 & 4.0, Animator Studio Pro, Realspace Panaroma Viewer, Smoothmove Panaroma

1600 International Drive, McLean, Virginia

View, Cosmo VRML Player from Silicon Graphics.

Drawing Process/Digital Technique:

Accurender is used with an AutoCAD-generated 3D model to create the 'raw' rendering (raster file). The image is 'finished' by using photo-montage, air-brushing, and other digital painting techniques in Adobe Photoshop.

Concept:

This 90,000 square-foot, four-story office building with one additional level of parking has been designed to be built over an existing three-level garage for an adjacent building. The main entry and tower feature face a major intersection. The design complements the adjacent building while presenting its own distinctive presence for the tenant. The design captures buildable square footage not used by the adjacent building in this desirable suburban location.

Credits:

Principal-in-Charge: Douglas N. Carter, AIA
Design Director: Thomas Dinneny
Project Director: Andrew C. Smith, AIA
Project Manager: Albert J. Thackrah, AIA
Digital Designers/Artists: Christopher L. Garwood, Nancy McCann-De Lalio

1600 International Drive, McLean, Virginia

099

Deiss and Associates with OLIVER + RAY Architects

Web Site: www.flash.net/~oliveray
E-mail: Oliveray@flash.net
Houston, Texas 77098

Urban Showroom
Automotive Flagship

Profile:

Oliver+Ray Architects are design consultants who affiliate with specialized architectural offices on a variety of national and international projects. Current work includes national retail prototypes for the automotive and restaurant industry. Oliver+Ray's work has been awarded and published nationally and locally, including a "Progressive Architecture" Award in 1997 from Architecture magazine. The two projects shown are design colaborations with Deiss and Associates of California.

Use of Digital Media:

The computer is integrated into the project from conception as both a design and communication tool. In the design process it is used to evaluate spatial, material and lighting concepts under consideration. These ideas are shared with consultants at various stages of development using digital images, animation, and vrml on the internet. Digital media (images and animations) are then incorporated with traditional drawing and physical models in presentations to the client.

Hardware:

Dual Pentium 166, 128 MB RAM, 1.5 gig hard drive, Zip Drive, Jaz Drive, 12x CD ROM, HP 4ML Printer, HP DesignJet 700 Plotter, 81/2 x 14 Scanner (MicroTek E3).

Software:

Windows NT 4.0, AutoCad R13, AutoCAD R13 Internet Publishing, Lightscape 3.1, Photoshop 4.0, Microsoft Explorer 4.0.

Drawing Process/ Imaging Technique:

Models are constructed in AutoCad, lighting and rendering are done in Lightscape, and texture maps are prepared in Photoshop. Animations are done using Lightscape and AutoCad utilities in combination with (.gif) animation utilities or Explorer 4.0 advertising banner utilities for publication on the internet.

Urban Showroom

Design Concept:

Urban Showroom: This project is an initial study for a small prototypical retail showroom for the introduction of a new automobile. It is to be constructed in pedestrian shopping zones in 12-15 Italian cities. Lighting and projection are key elements of the design allowing the environment to be continually transformed.

Automotive Flagship: The Flagship is a national prototype dealership developed for an international automotive manufacturer. It incorporates new technologies and concepts from non-automotive retail venues and presents them in elevation as a sectional idea. It is intended to be built in key U.S. markets and act as lighthouses for the manufacturer's entire dealer network. This project is hypothetical and intended to drive other facility types currently being designed for this client.

Automotive Flagship

Credits:

OLIVER + RAY Architects

Principals: Douglas Oliver, James Ray
Project Team: Mike King, Tony Hartin, Sarah Holbrook, Blair Satterfield, Mark Swackhamer
Computer image: Tony Hartin

Deiss and Associates

President: Hans Deiter Deiss
Project Manager: Greg Donald
Design Principal: Ken Nelson

101

Delphi Productions

Web Site: www.delphiproductions.com

Alameda, California 94501

AVE Exhibit Design, Washington, D.C.
Informix Tradeshow Booth

▌Profile:

Delphi Productions creates tradeshow exhibits and manages special events using the art of design and the craft of theater. Their services also include environmental, industrial, and graphic design, as well as theatrical productions. The selective clients includes Apple Computers, Ascend Communications, Sony, Novellus, and Oakland Museum. The firm has a staff of over 75 talented designers, project managers, and craftspeople.

▌Use of Digital Media:

At Delphi Productions the digital media plays a very significant role in all spectrum of design execution, from conceptual studies to final production. Following are the basic software that are used at various levels of the total process.

3D modeling : Form•Z rendering, MiniCad. Detail Drawing: MiniCad, AutoCad. Graphics: Adobe Photoshop, Adobe Illustrator, QuarkExpress. Output devices: HP laser printer, Epson Color printer, HP Plotter. Site survey, and documentation: Kodak Digital camera. Marketing: Powerpoint slide presentation. Project Management: Microsoft Word, File Maker Pro, Microsoft Excel.

Credits:
(AVE Exhibit Design)
Design: Anthony Erpelding, Kijeong Jeon
Rendering: Kijeong Jeon

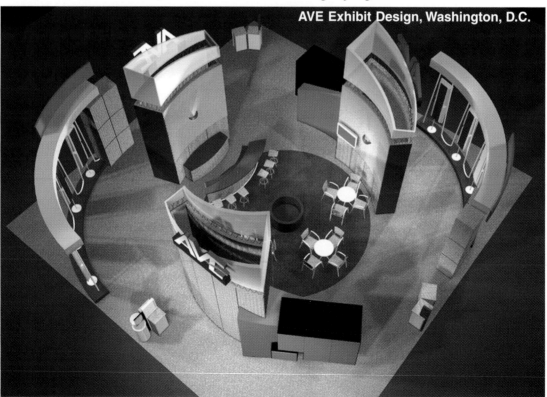

AVE Exhibit Design, Washington, D.C.

Hardware:

Power Macintosh G3 for modeling and rendering, and Epson Stylus Color printer for hard copy print out.

Software:

MiniCAD V.7, Form•Z Renderzone and Adobe Photoshop.

Drawing Process / Image Technique:

Hand-drawn sketches and diagrams were produced first to visualize the conceptual design of the project. Then 3D development and modeling were accomplished in MiniCad

v. 7. MiniCAD file was saved in DXF format and imported to Form•Z RenderZone for rendering effects. Color and material study were accomplished through digital rendering techniques. Effective lighting and color manipulation played an important role in creation of the final virtual photorealistic space. The rendered file was saved in TIFF format and import into the Adobe Photoshop program to add graphics and people for scale. Epson color printer was used for output in 11"X17" presentation format.

Credits:
(Informix Tradeshow Booth)
Design: Patrick Poinsot & Anthony Erpelding
Rendering: Kijeong Jeon

Informix Tradeshow Booth

Peter Edgeley

E-mail: p.edgeley@c031.aone.net.au

Australia

Taiwan Cinema and Retail Center

Profile:

Peter Edgeley qualified as an architect in the UK, but now works mainly as an illustrator and painter.

He has received awards at annual exhibitions of the ASAP in the USA and been an invited exhibitor with the illustrations society of Japan. He has also exhibited at the Royal College of Art at the UK as well as in his adapted home in Australia.

His work together as an architect and illustrator has received commendation at international level.

Use of Digital Media:

CAD is used to create a 3D model initially. A wireframe then forms the basis of a traditional rendering or a digital image. As the example shows the two can be interchangeable and are complementary.

Hardware:

Power Macintosh with 208 MB of RAM and A3 Wacom graphics tablet.

Software:

For CAD- "Design Workshop" due its rapid uncomplicated 3D construction and natural viewing controls. For Digital Manipulation- Photoshop. For Digital Drawing and Painting- Painter.

Drawing Process/Digital Technique:

The original daytime illustrations drawn and painted with conventional methods. It was then scanned and the following four steps show how the digital version was altered from day to night.

From day to night time view (refer to sketches):
1. Stretch sky using Photoshop effects scale.
2. Add black background and increase foliage to trees on either side. Use paint brush.
3. Selectively darken and increase contrast. Add evening

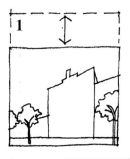 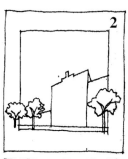

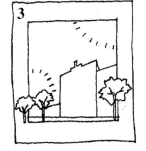 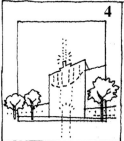

sky tones, i.e., ranging from deep blue to the warn ochres of sunset. Use airbrush gradient fills.
4. Add neon and lightening effects to a separate Photoshop layer. This allows great control over fine tuning. It also makes final design changes possible without affecting the background layer. Use line tools, airbrush paths.

Design Concept:

The building to hold a cinema and rental complex had minimal glazing to the front facade. It was a "black box" design, but was animated by a series of neon lines and curves. The client after seeing the daytime view wanted an illustration which showed how this would look at night.

Credits:

Architects: The Buchan Group, Melbourne
Project Architect: John Dennis
Design Architect: Chris Wood
Printing: A 'Lamba' continuous tone high gloss print from 'The Image Box,' Melbourne.

Einhorn Yaffee Prescott, Architecture & Engineering, P.C.

Web Site: www.eypae.com

New York, Washington, DC

Bala Cynwyd Middle School, Bala Cynwyd, Pennsylvania

Profile:

Einhorn Yaffee Prescott, Architecture & Engineering, P.C., (EYP) is a multi-disciplinary architecture, engineering, interior design, and technology firm with offices in Albany, White Plains, and New York, NY; Washington, DC; Boston, MA; and Los Angeles, CA. EYP has received over 100 national awards for design excellence.

Use of Digital Media at EYP:

EYP applies digital design tools toward a variety of ends. In initial presentations to new or prospective clients, the firm is able to showcase its early understanding of the client's needs, and allows the client an insight into EYP's integrated design approach. During project design development, EYP's architects and clients can interactively modify the building's digital representations to continually refine the design process, and demonstrate to the client the results of proposed modifications.

Hardware:

Pentium II 400 MHz processor 128 MB RAM, 8 MB AGP Video Adapter, 1024 x 768 Display Device, Windows NT Workstation 4.0 SP3 Operating System.

Software:

AutoCAD 14, Form•Z, RenderZone, 3D Studio, Adobe Photoshop

Drawing Process / Image Technique:

The process for creating any given computer model will vary by degree depending on the designer. Most of EYP's modeling is done with AutoCAD 14, Form•Z and 3D Studio, and rendered with 3D Studio or RenderZone. Adobe Photoshop is also used to apply further modifications and enhancements to the rendered image.

■ Concept:

The library media center should be the heart of the academic environment. At Bala Cynwyd Middle School, by infilling a central courtyard and featuring an existing classical facade, a truly unique space has been created. This space not only reflects on the past, but architecturally evokes its mission of disseminating information both traditionally as well as electronically.

■ Credits:

Principal-in-Charge: Arthur R. Kaplan, AIA, NCARB
Design Principal: Douglas B. Hyde, AIA
Designer/Interiors: Antonio H.Y. Yau
Project Architect: Thomas J. Kenney, RA
Interiors Coordinator: Dragana Vlatkovic
Computer Model: Robert McClure

Ellerbe Becket Inc.

Web Site: www.ellerbebecket.com

Minneapolis, Minnesota 55402

Kingdom Trade Center, Riyadh, Saudi Arabia
Confidentail Headquarters Competition, United Arab Emirates
Yonsei University Medical Center, Seoul, Korea

Profile:

Ellerbe Becket is a major architectural organization with over 800 employees in 14 offices around the world. It is a firm that combines a unity of purpose and shared values within a context of regional diversity. The projects cover virtually the entire spectrum of building types. The firm's philosophy and organizational structure allows designers sufficient independence so that no single style, ideology or personality is dominant.

Ten years ago Ellerbe Becket made a strong commitment to computer modeling as a design tool by equipping and training a group with a 3D software called AES. In the beginning the group consisted mostly of students who occupied an area and an attitude that became known as the Ghetto. Some have left EB since then and new folks have stepped in, but the core of this group remains at EB and are Stan Chiu, Mike Kennedy, Dave Koenen, and Jeff Walden. The projects below are an example of their cooperative hands in the process.

Ellerbe Becket's Use of Digital Media:

The design process always begins with the physical model. The group charettes with foam massing studies, increasing in scale until the medium becomes too cumbersome at which point a design direction has been determined, a vocabulary of materials suggested, and a language of shapes and forms spoken about, but indeterminate as to how they will fit together in a cohesive statement. These things are figured out on the computer which allows the group to develop and judge a design effectively and then move on. While each of the following projects had large and diverse design teams, the team members listed design in 3D CAD.

Hardware and Software:

Hardware: Micron Millennia Pro2, dual 200MHz processors.

Software: AES, AutoCAD, Form•Z, 3D Studio R3, Adobe Photoshop.

Design Concepts and Credits:

Kingdom Center:
The client, HRH Prince Alwaleed Bin Talal Bin Abdulaziz Alsaud, a private entrepreneur and international investor from Saudi Arabia desired that his building be a singular monolithic icon against the skyline of Riyadh, the profile of which could be described with a few swipes of the pen. The tower was developed to become a play of curves and planes intersecting each other resulting in elliptical residual space resolved by a delicately arching observation deck.
3D CAD Designers: Les Chylinski, Paul Davis, Rob Herrick, Dave Koenen, Chris Mullen, Phil Oliver, Mark Searls, Jeff Walden.

Confidential Headquarters Competition:
Within a major business center, this headquarters building was designed to rise as a world class institution responding to two very different scales. Within the context of the city skyline, the simple and dramatic profile of the tower massing would be memorable and instantly recognizable both day and night. At this distance, the tower's fenestration appears as the grain of pattern of a woven tapestry; its glass facades reflect the sky and the water, enlivening the building with the colors of nature. As the tower is approached, a new understanding of the building emerges. A stone framework cradles the glass column with bands or ribs holding the composition and uniting it with the garden base.
3D CAD Designers: Rob Herrick, Dave Koenen, Derek McCallum, Chris Mullen, Jeff Walden.

Yonsei University Medical Center:
Yonsei University Medical Center has been the largest private medical institution in Korea for over a century. The most challenging aspects of this project were designing a 1,006-bed hospital on a tight urban site and linking the existing campus with the new facilities -- all within a Korean government ordinance requiring designated areas not to exceed seven stories in height to avoid obstructing views from the city to the countryside.
3D CAD Designers: Stan Chiu , Paul Davis, Mic Johnson, Mike Kennedy, Kwang Bae Kim, Dave Koenen, Jeff Walden.

108

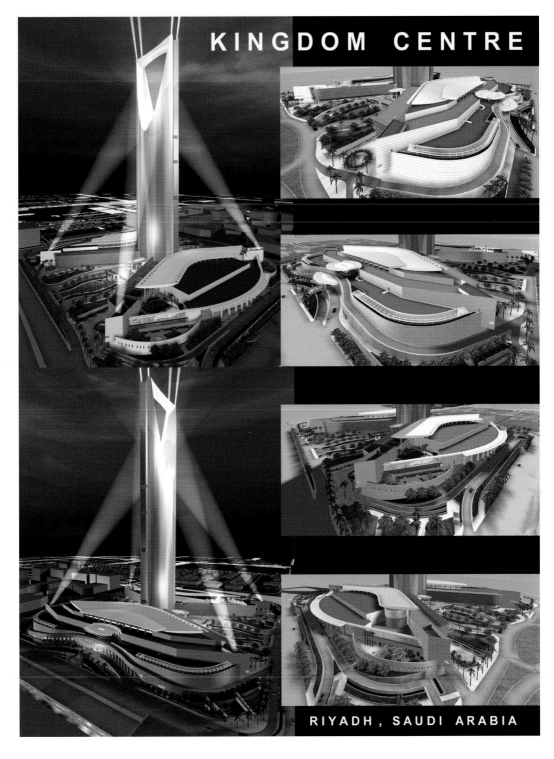

KINGDOM CENTRE

RIYADH, SAUDI ARABIA

competition:

round 1

round 2

round 3

Confidential Headquarters Competition

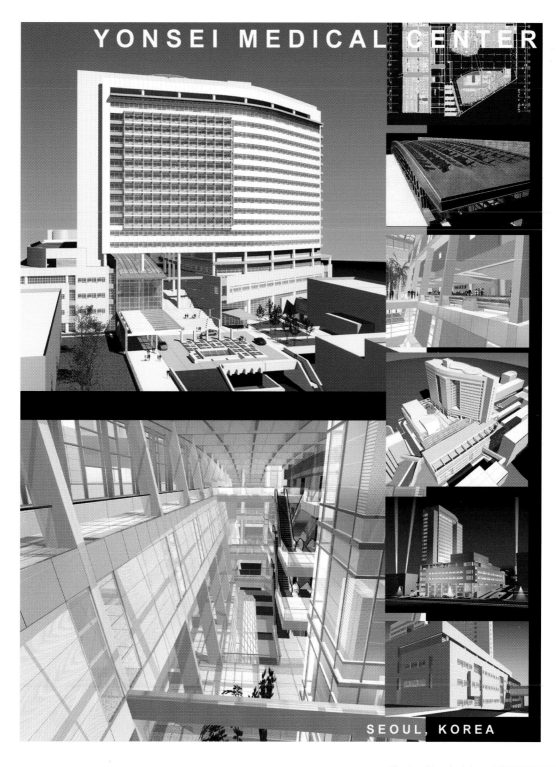

YONSEI MEDICAL CENTER

SEOUL, KOREA

Felderman + Keatinge Associates

Web Site: www.fkadesign.com
E-mail: fka@mindsprings.com

Santa Monica, California 90404

Apetito/II Restaurant, Tokyo, Japan
Shibuya Railroad Station, Tokyo, Japan

Profile:

Established in 1990, Felderman + Keatinge Associates has been built on the previous twenty years of the partners, projects and experience. The multi-disciplinary firm, which provides interior, graphic, industrial and environmental design and architectural services, has been recognized worldwide for its exquisitely-choreographed balance of witty, innovative designs and precise detailing for a distinguished roster of leading-edge clients. Among its clients are MTV Networks, Disney, Mattel, Samsung, Venini/Flos, Steelcase, Interface and Haworth.

Hardware and Software:

Hardware: Pentium II, 266 MHz, 128 MB ram. Epson and Kodak paper are used for final printing. For poster-like images, Hewlett Packard photo paper is used.

Software: Form•Z, 3D Studio Max, AutoCAD, Photoshop, PageMaker.

Drawing Process / Image Technique:

Two dimensional wire frames are done in AutoCAD and then imported into Form•Z to create 3D spaces. Final renderings are completed in 3D Studio Max. Final touches are done in Photoshop.

112

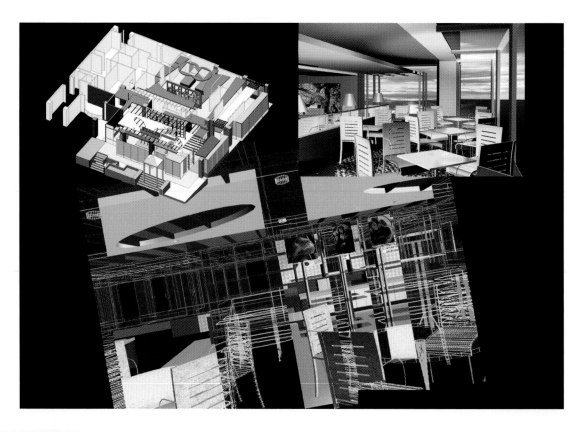

Concept:

Apetito: Apetito is a full service restaurant and bakery, displaying 100 different types of bread at all times. The design juxtaposes raw, unfinished structural elements against refined, natural finishes and materials.

Shibuya: The Shibuya Station project is situated on a 14,400 square-meter site. Stretching over seven city blocks, the structure is sandwiched into a narrow corridor, with strong street presence only on the east and west entrances. The building, which will link the commuter trains of three Japanese railway companies, is intended to serve the 60 million passengers who annually travel through this station 24 hours a day, seven days a week with five floors of restaurants and retail.

Credits:

Apetito/Il Restaurant, Tokyo, Japan: Stanley Felderman, Nancy Keatinge, Sandeep Sopori, Vishal Garg.

Shibuya Railroad Station, Tokyo, Japan: Stanley Felderman, Tom Ahn, Sandeep Sopori.

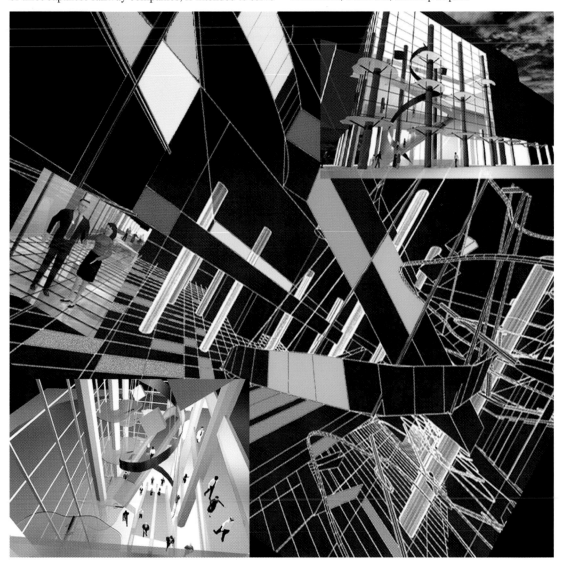

113

Form:uLA / Bryan Cantley + Kevin O'Donnell

E-mail: bcantley@fullerton.edu
kevinodonell@shookdesign.com

Santa Ana, California 92705, Los Angeles, California 90036

Big Foot, NSL Stadium Competition, Santa Monica, California
CSUF Art Gellery, California State University Fullerton, California

Profile:

Form:uLA is a virtual design studio, with energies devoted to both theoretical and built architecture; graphic communication and propaganda; installations; and interpretations of movement through form. The two partners, do not occupy the same physical geography, but instead collaborate through cyberspace.

Use of Digital Media:

Form:uLA uses digital media both as a design tool as well as a production tool. They are interested in using software intentionally for purposes not originally intended. The partners use the digital media as a means of communication and design review in response to separate locations. They are developing a methodology that involves an oscillation of hardware, software, and traditional techniques that do not place any one medium as the "production" tool.

Hardware:

Macintosh Power PC, Exacto-knife, pen.

Software:

Strata Studio Pro, Form•Z, Photoshop, QuarkXPress.

Drawing Process / Image Technique:

Both drawings were done as hybrid images that involved several layers. Each "pass" at each different location for the image manipulation was done by alternating programs. Some forms were constructed by hand through sketch and study model; built in Form•Z and re-manipulated in Strata [and vice-versa]; altered and composite layered in Photoshop and Quark [which are used as compilation devices as well as digital painting and construction tools].

Concept:

Bigfoot:
A kinetic NFL Stadium that employs rotating seating. The bleacher section facing the Santa Monica Beach rotates 180 degrees to view water sports and activities when football is not being played. Shown is the interior installation of the Bar/Restroom facility in a typical luxury box.

CSUF Gallery:
Entry to an existing Fine Arts Gallery that deals with the paradoxical situation of evaluating art work based on cash sales. Shown is a composite worm's-eye showing assemly additions only, superimposed with details from announcement panels.

Credits:

Form:uLA / Bryan Cantley + Kevin O'Donnell
Model assistants: Treva Kuyper, Kevin Kennedy, Terry Vickers

114

Big Foot

CSUF Gallery

csuf gallery one : panel o1 ©

5 13831 41797 1

Fox & Fowle Architects

Web Site: www.foxfowle.com
E-mail: info@foxfowle.com

New York, New York

The Reuters Building, Three Times Square, New York, New York

▍Profile:

Fox & Fowle Architects is an architectural, interior design and planning firm of 55 people, based in New York City. Robert F. Fox, Jr. and Bruce S. Fowle formed Fox & Fowle Architects in 1978. The essential character of the firm's work is aptly described in the words the American Institute of Architects wrote to present Bruce Fowle to its College of Fellows: the "work is distinct and unique; the reliance on form, proportion and detail has achieved warmth and a sense of place. This basic, purist approach to design will allow it to endure." Long before the term "green" entered the popular lexicon, Fox & Fowle has maintained a commitment to environmentally responsible design and to the integration of the principles of sustainable architecture into every aspect of our professional practice.

▍Fox & Fowle's Use of Digital Media:

Fox & Fowle has been using computer aided design (CAD) technology since 1986. A strong commitment to the integration of this tool into the firm's design and production processes has allowed this system to grow into more than 20 advanced CAD workstations, all part of the firms local area network of more than 55 computers. CAD technol-ogy is applied through every phase of architectural design and construction document production. Digital zoning studies and area analyses become 3D massing models and spatial studies, which in turn are developed into computer rendered presentations. CAD data files and other electronic data communications are exchanged with clients, consultants, and contractors via email, disk exchange, and our in-house bulletin-board system. A T-1 link to the Internet provides a high speed connection to the World Wide Web from every desktop in the office.

▍Hardware / Software:

Hardware: Typical CAD workstations are equipped with Pentium II 400MHz processors and 128MB RAM, running under the Windows NT 4.0 operating system. All users have access to flatbed and slide scanners, and large and small format color printers.

Software: AutoCAD R14, with AEC Tools, is core CAD software. Additionally Photoshop, Accurender, MColor, Quark, and 3D Studio are utilized for digital media production.

The Reuters Building, Three Times Square, NY

The Reuters Building, Three Times Square, New York

Drawing Process/ Digital Technique:

Models were created from construction documents in AutoCAD and rendered in Accurender. Additional modeling done in Trispectives. Photoshop used for image enhancement and correction.

Concept:

The new Reuters Building on Seventh Avenue and 42nd Street will occupy a pivotal point at the Crossroads of the World. Serving as a crucial link between the famous Times Square bow-tie area to the north and the newly revitalized 42nd Street theatre and entertainment district to the west. Its charge is to be both a corporate icon and a dynamic fulcrum that draws visual energy from

each. Fox & Fowle Architects has designed a building that has both the stature and elegance of a corporate headquarters and the populist appeal of Times Square's unrestrained commercialism.

Credits:

Robert Fox, Bruce Fowle, Daniel Kaplan, Elizabeth Finkelshteyn
Digital Image: Zheng Dai and Brian Davison

117

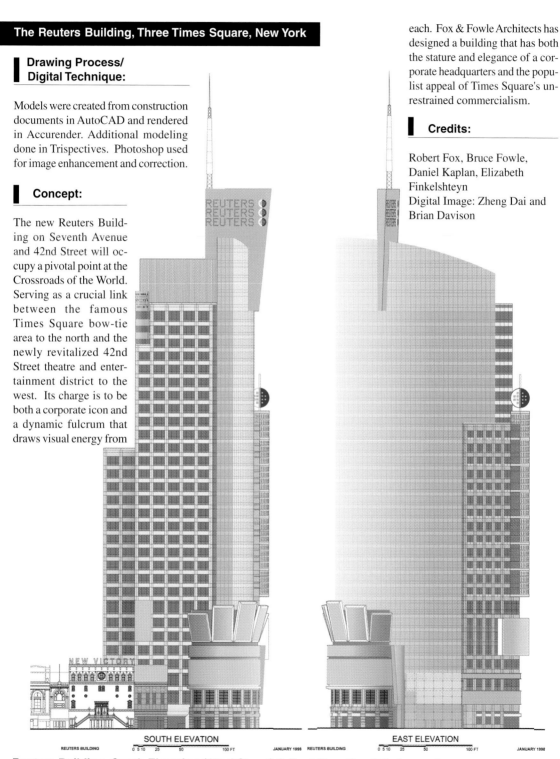

SOUTH ELEVATION
REUTERS BUILDING   0 5 10   25   50   100 FT   JANUARY 1998

EAST ELEVATION
REUTERS BUILDING   0 5 10   25   50   100 FT   JANUARY 1998

Reuters Building: South Elevation (42nd Street) & East Elevation (7th Avenue)

Carl Hampson

Web: www.hippo.cc

Los Angeles, California 90036

DE-CENTERING "Centering the Civic" San Francisco, California

Profile:

Carl Hampson teamed with Oscillation Digital Design in San Francisco with the common goal of integrating emerging information technologies with the development of architecture. Their collaborative investigations yielded theoretical projects which attempted to coexist within both virtual and actual environments. Their breakthrough project, De-Centering, was awarded in the 1996 San Francisco Prize Competition. As a project designer at SMP-SHG Architects in Los Angeles, Carl was able to apply this design approach to the development of "real" projects. His design for a corporate data center was both inspired and informed by the use of digital media. He recently co-founded Independent Architects where he continues to evolve a design approach rooted in technology.

Use of Digital Media:

Computer generated 3D visualization is used from the onset of each project. Sketches are quickly transformed into virtual study models. Client presentations are prepared utilizing desktop publishing software in addition to graphic layouts which inspire design ideas and evolve a studio identity. A variety of programs are utilized which enhance design, production and presentation.

Hardware:

Macintosh Power PC 7300 200 MHz, 96 MB RAM, 1.2 GB hard drive, 17" Toshiba Monitor.
IBM compatible Pentium 166 MHz, 64 MB RAM, 1.6 GB hard drive, 17" Toshiba monitor.

Software:

AutoCad Release 13, Form•Z Renderzone 2.8, Adobe Photoshop 4.0, Adobe Illustrator 6.0, Adobe Streamline.

Drawing Process / Image Technique:

Design sketches were converted to vector drawings with Adobe Streamline. Team members transformed these drawings into 3D models working on discreet components

of the project on various platforms in both Form•Z and AutoCad. The final model was assembled and rendered in Form•Z Renderzone. Presentation layouts were assembled in Adobe Illustrator.

Concept:

De-Centering is a critique of current cultural transitions, a study in how new architectures might exist with the extreme technological flux of the information age. Two components suggest alternate scales of social interaction. The project suggests an architectural idiom identifying San Francisco as the creative center of digital technology, an industry almost transparent to the world. The elements of BRIDGE and BEACON are prosthetics, architectural "cybernetics" introduced to create a new public space greater than the sum of its parts.

Credits:

Carl Hampson, Brian Kralyevich, Andy Drake, Brian O'Driscoll
Oscillation Digital Design
Design and Graphics

DE-CENTERING "Centering the Civic" San Francisco, California

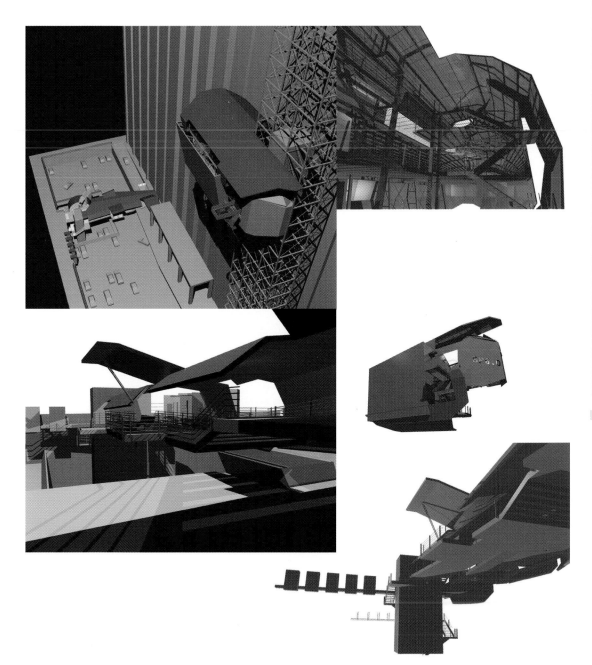

HDR Architecture, Inc.

Web: www.hdrinc.com

Omaha, Nebraska

Bakersfield Heart Hospital, Bakersfield, California
Princess Margaret Hospital, Swindon, England

Profile:

Founded in 1917, HDR is a nationwide, full-service professional practice staffed with architects, engineers, planners and interior designers with 39 offices nationwide. Specializing in healthcare design for more than 30 years, design centers located in Omaha, Nebraska; Chicago, Illinois; Alexandria, Virginia; and Dallas, Texas have designed more than 500 healthcare design commissions nationwide and abroad for more than 200 clients. HDR Architecture also has been recognized as a national leader and award-winning design firm of justice facilities as well as supporting the advancement of technology by providing design solutions for world-renowned universities, corporations and government institutions.

HDR's Use of Digital Media:

HDR uses digital media extensively in various modes including: design synthesis; design presentation; animations; web-page authoring; marketing proposals, brochures and reports. The firm is gradually moving toward the 'single building model' approach which will integrate the tools for 2D and 3D visualization throughout the entire design and production process.

Hardware and Software:

Hardware: PC based Pentium II 333 MHz.
Software: Microstation SE, Masterpiece and Triforma, TrueSpace 3.1, Adobe Photoshop, Corel Draw 8.

Bakersfield Heart Hospital, Bakersfield, California

Drawing Process / Image Technique:

Floor plans and sections are drawn in 2D and rendered with color fills. Elevations, site plans and 3D views are extracted from the 3D model rendered with shadows, textures and transparency. Image manipulation is accomplished in Photoshop. Final sheet composition and/or page layout is done in Corel Draw. Color printed output may be slides, 8.5 x 11 FUJI pictograph prints, 11 x 17 Fiery prints on Canon PS-IPU Laser or large format HP 2500 inkjet plots. Special renderings may be plotted high resolution photographic quality in large format as well.

Concept:

This modern health care building facilitates a unique concept of high tech, patient focused services. Conceived as a prototype building, the primary challenge was in responding to a regional context of 'competitive' imagery. Therefore a central glass entry tower rises up to become a 'beacon' to the community and signal the presence of this specialized service. The use of CADD was instrumental in depicting the 'feel' of an all glass entrance lobby, as well as show the amount of solar penetration that occurs on the north facing building.

Credits:

Project Manager: Randall Hood.
Designer: Mike Tangney.

Princess Margaret Hospital, Swindon, England

Drawing Process / Image Technique:

TrueSpace provided the designers with a real-time immersive feedback during form creation, where expedited design decisions resulted in an enhanced and complete aesthetic form, appropriate for the project. The immersive approach to design methodology encouraged a holistic approach where a feed back loop was in use. This process allowed the form, effected the plan, and plan effected the form, as in symbiotic relationship.

Concept:

The building layout was influenced by the idea of allowing natural ventilation and natural lighting into all patients' rooms. An innovative design integrated American health care delivery concepts with British health care practice. The overall building form was spread out to limit height, with the vertical stair shafts placed at the end of each corridor to anchor the form.

Credits:

Project Management: Bill Palmer, Clark Miller
Design: John Cameron, Loren Lamprecht, Patrick Leahy
Computer Imagery: F. Kholousi

Bakersfield Heart Hospital, California

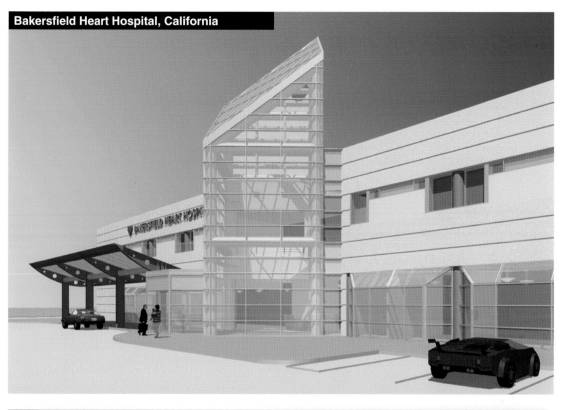

Princess Margaret Hospital, Swindon, England

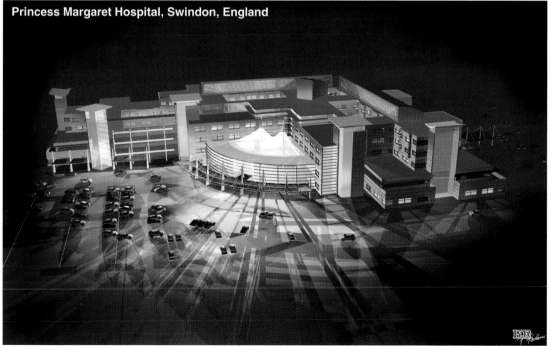

121

HLW International

e-mail: kbarclay@hlw.com
Web:www.hlw.com
New York, New York 10003

International Trade Center, Seoul, Korea

Profile:

HLW International is a world renowned design firm providing comprehensive services in architecture, engineering, interiors, planning, and landscape design. With a staff of more than 265 professionals headquartered in New York City and a history that spans more than a century, the depth and diversity of our capabilities are the cornerstones of our practice.

HLW was founded in 1885 by architect Cyrus L.W. Eidlitz, who joined forces with engineer Andrew McKenzie in 1900 to form the partnership Eidlitz & McKenzie. Since those early days, the firm has continued to make its mark: first as one of the original architects of the New York City skyline with such projects as the New York Times Building in 1905, and 1 Wall Street or The Irving Trust Building in 1931. Today HLW continues to lead with pioneering planning and design projects for Fox Broadcasting Company, The Walt Disney Company, ABC Television, Schering Plough Corporation, Rupert Murdoch's News Corporation Ltd., the New York Stock Exchange, and other prestigious clients.

HLW's Use of Digital Media:

HLW employs digital media from project conception through development to final documentation and delivery.

Hardware:

The firm uses a PC network for all disciplines which is connected to our branch offices in Los Angeles, San Francisco, London and Shanghai. Printing is done to high resolution large and small format color plotters and laser printers.

Software:

The firm uses Microstation for 2D drafting and 3D modeling as well as Softimage for 3D modeling and animation. Photoshop, QuarkXPress, and Illustrator are used for graphic design.

Drawing Process / Image Technique:

Initial design concepts and massing are developed, modeled, and rendered in Microstation and Softimage. Depending on the project the firm employs raytracing in Microstation SE or mental ray in Softimage for final renderings. Through the use of photo-montage these projects are often placed in their site with Photoshop.

Concept:

Design studies were initiated using Softimage massing models as well as with physical models. As the design developed 2D Microstation plans and sections were used to confirm precise program requirements and dimensions. These were imported back into Softimage to then develop highly articulated structural components and curtain wall details. The complex curvature shapes and geometries were most easily modeled using nurb surfaces in Softimage. Text, characters, and articulation generated in Photoshop, Microstation and Illustrator were texture-mapped onto the surfaces of the glass curtain walls.

Credits:

HLW International
Partner-in-Charge: Leevi Kiil
Design Partner: Paul Boardman
Senior Designer: Arnold Lee
Project Manager: Dong Chan-Shin
Digital Model: Michael Isner

International Trade Center, Seoul, Korea

International Trade Center, Seoul, Korea

HNTB Architecture

e-mail: see web site
Web: www.hntb.com

Alexandria, Virginia 22314

Salt Lake City International Airport, Salt Lake City, Utah

Profile:

HNTB provides comprehensive planning and architectural design services to public and private clients throughout the United States and around the world. The firm's work has won local, regional and national awards for excellence in design. A significant focus of the practice has been Transportation Architecture with experience in Airport Planning and Design dating to 1944. Since that time, the firm has helped develop more than 150 airports, including international airports at Atlanta, Miami, Vancouver, Orlando, Boston and Washington, DC.

HNTB's Use of Digital Media:

Using technologically advanced media, HNTB explores project design parameters with the digital representation most appropriate to the specific idea. In early design stages, digital images are used to show concepts, diagrams and project component relationships. Both abstractly expressive and realistic images are developed as internal study and external communications tools. Other digital media are utilized to show complex analysis, systems coordination and planning overlays. Digital graphic montage is used extensively in presentation to indicate the complex layering of information inherent in every design project.

Hardware:

The office uses IBM-based PC's, large-format color plotters, medium-format, high-resolution printers, scanners and digital cameras. Servers connect every employee through a LAN system enabling communications, internet connection and file sharing. All HNTB offices are connected through a WAN allowing e-mail communication and electronic file transfer. HNTB maintains a firm web site, and web sites dedicated to individual projects. Secured areas in these sites, allow for sharing of drawing files with other consultants.

Software:

Windows NT based programs including AutoCAD and Microstation for two-dimensional drafting, AutoCAD and Form•Z for three dimensional modeling, 3D Studio Max and RenderZone for 3-dimensional renderings and animation, Adobe Photoshop, Adobe Illustrator and Quark for image manipulation and graphic organization, and PowerPoint for interactive computer presentations.

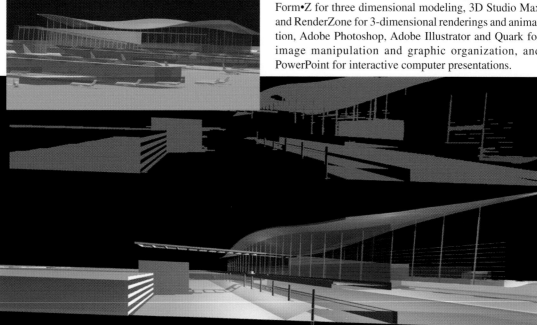

124

▌Drawing Process / Image Technique:

The drawings presented represent three distinct conceptual design approaches for the Salt Lake City International Airport. Based upon common plan forms and masses, the imagery presents an expressive impression of the architectural concepts. They vary in formal language and in their relationship to regional context, and include a fluid concept indicative of progress and abstract abstract reinvention, an elegant, simple geometry representing the stability of the original Utah settlements and an angular expression with indigenous coloration and naturalistic materials. By varying levels of coloration, transparency and articulation, the salient points of each design approach are emphasized at a subjective perceptual level. These types of images are frequently combined with more objective representations, for client and public presentation formats.

▌Credits:

Architect: HNTB Architecture
Assoc. Architect: Gensler
Principal in Charge: Steve Reiss
Design Principal: J. Lee Glenn
Senior Designers: Vlastamil Poch, Jennifer Swee, Benjamin Ames
Design Team: Clint Larkan, Jose Fioretto, Jose Atienza, Christine Mueller, Andrew Ellsworth, Mark Hutto

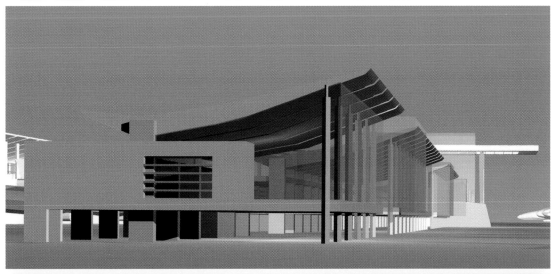

125

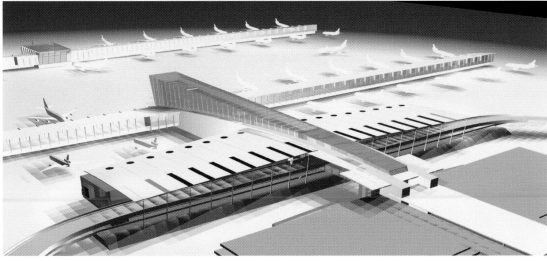

House + House Architects

E-mail: house@ix.netcom.com

San Francisco, California 94109

The Old Grandview Estate, Oakland, California

Profile:

Steven and Cathi House and their associates endeavor to create beauty, serenity and awe in their work. They find their greatest inspiration in the subtleties of each site and in the deepest recesses of their clients' souls. Through intimate analysis, they discover how to mold each project into a unique, magical and harmonious environment. They treat each project as an opportunity to lift themselves and their clients to a higher level of perception and enjoyment of the world...not through the latest technology, but through the skillful manipulation of form, light and texture. The poetic quality of their work derives from the simpler side of life: the magic sparkle of sunlight raking across a textured wall, the drama of surprise in turning a corner, the luminous glow of color at the moment of twilight...

Use of Digital Media:

The use of digital media occurs after the project has developed conceptually in the schematic design phase. Archicad allows immediate massing and spatial models to be rendered for the client's review. Final presentations are developed as the project draws to a close.

Hardware:

House + House uses Macintosh Power Mac computers to perform all of their digital needs. Output and scanning devices include an Epson Stylus color 1520 printer and a Umax flatbed scanner.

Software:

For their digital graphic and architectural work, House + House uses Archicad 6.0 for complete project modeling and rendering, Photoshop 4.0 for visual and graphic enhancement, and QuarkXPress 3.32 for presentation layout.

Drawing Process / IDigital Technique:

Although the actual design and production process for the Old Grandview Estate took place on the drawing boards, this project was selected for the purpose of exploring specific digital graphic/presentation techniques. The building was modeled in Archicad 6.0. Multiple perspective renderings were explored to discover the most informative and intricate views. The rendered images were transferred into Photoshop 4.0 to enhance the colors and quality. In QuarkXPress 3.32 a specific page size was created along with a geometric layout for precision and order. Saved in an EPS file for ease of transition, the images were moved from Photoshop into QuarkXPress, placed within the graphic format and text was added.

Concept:

Designed to celebrate the union of family, a place of refuge, growth and love, this new 4,000 square foot home resulted from the client's tragic loss in Oakland's 1991 firestorm. Sun, wind and views were studied, and the energy flows and spiritually powerful zones within the site were explored to incorporate concepts of feng shui and geomancy. Curving walls, deep set windows, rich colors and carefully proportioned spaces embrace a home with meaning in every move.

Credits:

Partner in Charge: Cathi House
Design Team: Cathi House, Steven House AIA, Michael Baushke
Digital Rendering: Shawn Brown

The Old Grandview Estate, Oakland, California

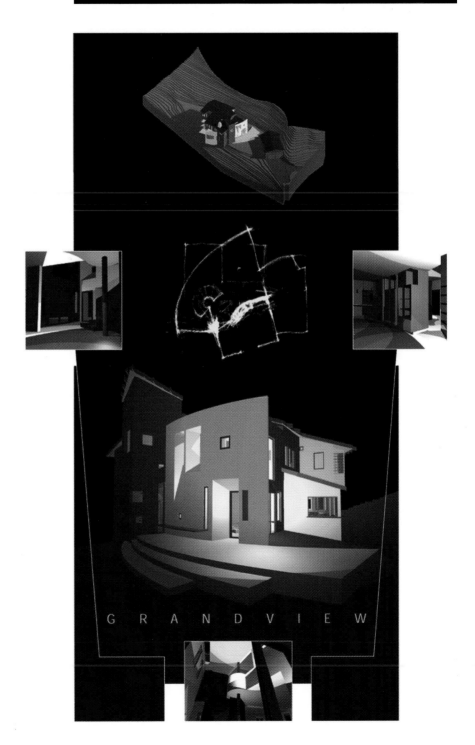

Inglese Architecture

E-Mail: Inglese@aol.com

San Francisco, California 94133

Drury Residence, New House, San Francisco, California

Profile:

Inglese Architecture is a young design firm located in San Francisco's Jackson Square District. The firm is dedicated to fine residential, commercial and civic architectural and interior design.

Mark English and associates Jeff Gard and Star Jennings follow a team-leader approach to design wherein talented artisans and builders are involved as collaborators from the beginning of the design process through construction.

Use of Digital Media in the Office:

All design and construction documents produced in the office are digitally created or manipulated. An integrated 3-D modeling and 2-D production drawing program is used for all projects. Scanned images are imported and melded with computer renderings for public agency review.

Hardware:

Macintosh G3 266 MHz with 6 GB hard drive and 96 MB RAM, Umax scanner, Epson printer.

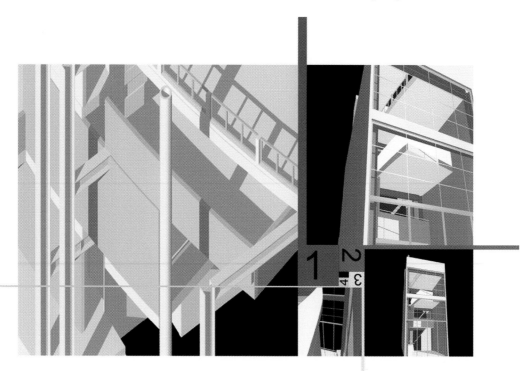

128

Software:

Archicad Teamwork 5.0, Photoshop 3.0, PageMaker 6.0.

Drawing Process/Digital Technique:

3-D models were created within Archicad using the Archicad rendering engine. The drawings were saved as PICT files and manipulated in Photoshop. Final arrangement of the drawing elements was achieved in PageMaker.

Design Concept:

The drawings are designed to show elements of the building in two modes: the first using perspective that imply a human point of view in vignette, the second using paraline drawings to express an analytical investigation of parts.

Credits:

Mark English, Jeff Gard, Star Jennings

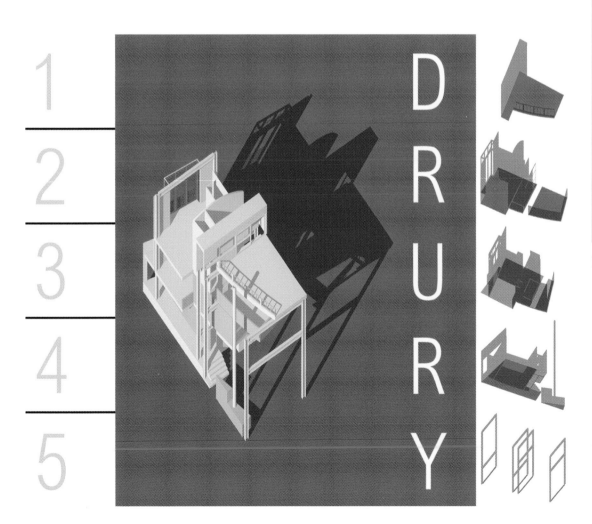

129

Murphy/Jahn

Chicago, Illinois 60601

Deutsche Post AG Bonn
Bayer AG Headquarters
Transrapid

▌ Profile:

The firm's work is based on the continued belief in constructional, rational, and technological determinants. These factors shape a building's systems and components along a logical and objective analysis, but architecture as a logical process alone is impossible. Above all, the firms attitudes follow a renewed interest in form and its resultant meaning and symbolism as a reaction against the mindless, continued applications of modernist (and post-modernist) principles - a reaction against modernism's "ultimate and unforgivable sin - the loss of style" (Huxtable).

This architecture represents a continuum and evolution from a strict functionalist, technological approach toward a synthesizing activity. The buildings deal with image, but also deal with function-plan, structure, and services. It is in synthesizing these that the designs draw upon pursuits characterized as formal (geometry, surface treatment, ornament), intellectual (meaning, metaphor, symbol), and social (resource consciousness and context in time and place, as well as people's use and perception of buildings).

These efforts represent a new architectural synthesis of abstract representation. They combine the rational clarity of abstractionism and technology with an interest in symbolism. They explore the relationship between function, construction and the resultant architectural form. They also explore the tension between art and technology in architecture.

▌ Use of the digital media in the office:

Murphy/Jahns digital tools are integrated with the design process. Digital modeling and rendering are employed in the earliest stages of concept development as a tool to evaluate and refine design options. While frequently used for presentation, the developmental value is primary. The goal of these renderings therefore is to capture the essential qualities of form, surface, transparency, environment and symbolism, rather than highly detailed photorealistic representation. CADD is viewed as much more than a fast electronic pencil. On projects where appropriate, animation techniques are used in a similar way.

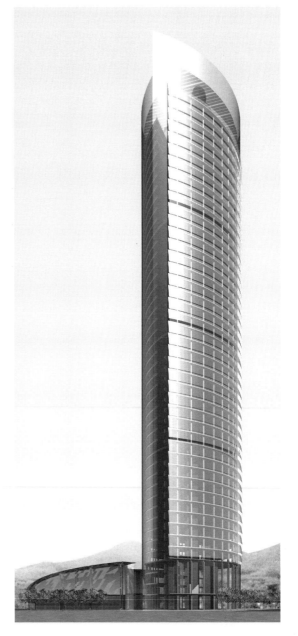

130

Hardware:

All modeling and rendering is done on PCs with Intel Pentium II technology running Windows NT or Windows 95. Large format (36x ~) monochrome output using an ocè 9800, and small format (12x18) color output using Fiery RIP and Canon CLC1000 are done in-house. Large format Iris prints are used when appropriate.

Software:

See Drawing Process/Image Technique under each project.

Project: Deutsche Post AG Bonn

Drawing Process / Image Technique:

The composite poster was created using a combination of 3D Modeling, 2D Drawing, Raster Paint, and Desktop Publishing Techniques. The Tower model was created in Microstation 95. Rendering was created using Microstation Masterpiece with Ray Tracing. Site plan and floor plans were drawn with AutoCad R14 and composed using PageMaker.

Design Concept:

The Deutsche Post project reinvents the tower office building type through the integration of urban design, function, technology and energy comfort. The split and shifted football plan shape connects the city to the Rhine river while providing daylight to the interior of the building and fulfilling the desire for social spaces in the form of skygardens within the project.

Encapsulating the building in a twin shell facade reduces energy use and maximizes daylight, resulting in an aesthetic of transparency, light and reflection.

Credits:

Helmut Jahn
Rendering: T.J. McLeish and John Manaves

Project: Bayer AG Headquarters

▌Drawing Process / Image Technique:

The 3D Model was created using 3D Studio Max R2 also used for rendering. Photographic context and entourage were created with a hybrid of modeled objects and raster images composed with the rendered image in Photoshop.

▌Design Concept:

This project, a new headquarters for the Bayer AG, is located adjacent to a large park in the corporate campus. The building replaces a much larger 1970's high-rise, a change reflecting the evolving requirements of the workplace and the corporate image. The new design creates an efficient, high density, composition of modern technologies, both in the format of office systems and building components, as opposed to the generalized loft spaces of previous office designs.

The entry is defined by a high pergola canopy, which is presented as a constructed landscape element. While functioning urbanistically to define the streetwall and maintain symmetry at the streetscape, the canopy also requires that those approaching the building pass through landscaping, reinforcing the sense that the building is situated within the park setting. Appropriate to this location, the entire building wall is composed of glass, allowing the distinction of interior and exterior to be very loose. Internal balcony terraces bring a further dissolution of the perceived barrier.

▌Credits:

Helmut Jahn
Rendering: Alphonso Peluso

*Perspektive
Eingangshalle*

Project: Transrapid

Drawing Process / Image Technique:

These images were modeled and rendered using 3D Studio Max R2. The sleek aerodynamic forms and polished/reflective/transparent surfaces employed in the design to express the high-speed aspects of the project are captured particularly well with this medium.

Design Concept:

The project includes development of prototype for 5 sta-tions serving the high speed Mag-Lev train system. The reduced and transparent construction with its long cantilevering roof, is symbolic of levitation and the high speed of the train. The adaptation of the prototype to the other stations was limited less by the suggested system than by the conditions of the different locations. The main interest is based on engineering and performance in contrast to design and styling. So the stations show their materials and construction as a clear diagram.

Credits:

Helmut Jahn
Rendering: Alphonso Peluso

TRANSRAPID

TRANSRAPID   HAMBURG-MOORFLEET

The Jerde Partnership International Inc.

E-mail: postmaster@jerde.com
Web Site: www.jerde.com

Venice, California 90291

Roppongi Subway Station, Tokyo, Japan

Profile:

Founded in 1977 and based on the innovative, humanistic vision and ideas of Jon Adams Jerde, FAIA, The Jerde Partnership International (JPI) designs large-scale, mixed-use projects that solidify a sense of place and identity for cities worldwide. The 130-member team speaks a design language that combines functionality with impact, inspiring an altogether new understanding of urbanism, community and the ongoing global evolution toward connectivity.

Use of Digital Media:

JPI's visualization philosophy incorporates the computer as a flexible, synergistic design tool. The firm creates large-scale, mixed-use projects that solidify a sense of place; its ideas explore and enhance the user's experience. In this context, digital media make more effective the study of complex spatial relationships. The firm and its clients better understand how the completed "place" looks and feels with this view inside the project.

Hardware:

Desktop workstations: Dual 350 MHz processors, 256 MB RAM, 16 MB graphics card. Single 266 MHz processors, 164 MB RAM, 8 MB graphics card. LAN, Sun Microsystems network (i + terabyte), Raid Level 5.

Software:

AutoCAD v. 14, 3D Studio Max v. 2.5, Razor Mach Pro 4, Perception VR Player, After Effects, Photoshop, Corel Draw. Plug ins: Max Matter, Surface Tools, Tree Factory, Kai's Power Tools.

Drawing Process / Image Technique:

The JPI process begins simultaneously in two and three dimensions. Schematic plans, which are based on programming and other requirements, are sculpted and manipulated formally in three dimensions. The designers then proceed to work non-linearly, cutting sections from models and extruding two-dimensional into three-dimensional work. As the design develops, details are layered onto the model. Final renderings then move to Photoshop for touch up and added realism.

Design Concept:

Roppongi, Tokyo, Japan.
The large-scale, mixed-use urban district on 28.4 acres in Tokyo is being designed to enhance and expand the definition, identity and cohesion of the existing Roppongi area. The design inspirations which are being explored are found in the site itself and are defined by the changes to be experienced from low park to high urban, from the historical park to the high cultural state of man's built environment. The subway station is designed to become the new identity icon and arrival point.

Credits:
The Jerde Partnership International Inc.
Image: Matthew Baran

Kajima Corporation

Web Site: www.kajima.co.jp

Tokyo, Japan

Office Building, Tokyo, Japan
NEOLAB project
DIB-200 project

Profile:

Twenty years after its establishment in 1840, Kajima Corporation constructed Japan's first Western-style building-the Eiichibankan-in Yokohama. Since then, Kajima has rapidly developed its operations by anticipating future trends in all types of construction-related needs. The company's activities have encompassed the railway construction and electric power development that propelled Japan's initial modernization as well as the coastal industrial developments, high-rise structures, nuclear power plants, and maritime-related projects that helped the nation rise quickly to economic superpower status. Today, as one of Japan's leading construction companies Kajima maintains subsidiaries in North America, Europe, and Asia and is active in construction and real estate development businesses around the world. With an eye to the dynamic changes under way in the operating and social environment, Kajima will continue to evolve, supported by superior technological expertise, rich human resources, and a pioneer spirit.

Kajima's Use of Digital Media:

Kajima has succeeded in integrating digital media into the design process. Many of Kajima designers have achieved a true paperless technique, where concepts take shape on 3D modelers without the use of a single sketch. Part of this achievement is due to Kajima's excellent computer resources, but more importantly the lofty goal of creating a total digital building must take the credit. With Kajima it isn't enough to have output in the form of drawings, images and animations, but the actual building itself should be the digital output. To support this, Kajima has been active in training designers to use digital media in the design stage, has utilized techniques for digital manufacturing and has developed and built robots and automated construction machines for the erection of real buildings from digital models.

Hardware:

Kajima began with IBM mainframes which were replaced with networked IBM RS-6000 workstations. The examples shown were designed using the RS-6000's, however most Kajima designers have recently moved to Macintosh or PC. Output devices include Pictrography color digital printer, vector / rastor electrostatic plotter and laser printers.

Software:

The examples shown were designed using CATIA and rendered with REALS (developed inhouse). Photomontage includes Shimatronix and Photoshop. Current designer's choice for software include Form•Z and Renderzone among others.

Office Building, Tokyo, Japan

Drawing Process / Image Technique:

Computer generated line drawing with a rendering perspective view. Early in the design process a sheet was composed on CATIA which comprised of various "windows" opening up onto the 3D model. Design proceeded from a blank screen and consisted of manipulating and analyzing CATIA solids. With each variation, the "windows" on the sheet automatically generate two-dimensional drawings. 3D solid model was produced on CATIA during the design process. Rendering was completed on inhouse "REALS" ray tracing software. Drawings printed out on electrostatic plotter Output format includes digitally produced print, slide and 4x5 positive.

Design Concept:

Floors two through four function as a library, with offices on floors five through seven. The front of the building responds to the street with conventional curtain wall construction while the entire rear facade becomes a truss wall containing core elements: elevators, exterior stairways, restroom modules, and exposed mechanical equipment. Angular study nooks portrude through the truss wall on the library floors.

Credits:

Kajima Corporation, Japan
Design: A. Scott Howe and Tomohito Okudaira
Digital Drawing: A Scott Howe

Office Building, Tokyo, Japan

NEOLAB project

Drawing Process/Image Technique:

3D solid model was produced on CATIA during the design process. Rendering was completed on inhouse "REALS" ray tracing software. Photomontage by Shimatronix graphics paint systems.

Design Concept:

Various research functions surround a central spherical atrium space, with the lower hemisphere forming a negative cavity below grade and the upper hemisphere having the form of a dome. The crystalline dome reflects the beauty of the surrounding sky, greenery and ocean and incorporates functions which capture solar energy. The atrium serves as a link to the surrounding community with exhibits and demonstrations of current research projects on public display.

Credits:

Kajima Corporation, Japan
Design: A. Scott Howe
Digital Drawing: Mika Ogouchi

NEOLAB project

DIB-200 project

Drawing Process/Image Technique:

Computer graphics sectional perspective rendering. 3D solid model was produced on CATIA during the design process. Rendering was completed on inhouse "REALS" ray tracing software. Photomontage by Shimatronix graphics paint systems.

Design Concept:

A 1,500,000m2 (16,148,000sf) office / residential / hotel 200 floor, 800m high super highrise building. The building includes 320 residential units and 2,500 hotel rooms and supports an occupancy load of 40,000 to 50,000. Twelve 50-story cylindrical units are assembled in the form of four towers connected by a super girder skeletal structural system. Sky lobbies coinciding with the super girders provide platforms for express elevator platforms, heliports and access to local elevator systems.

Credits:

Kajima Corporation, Japan
Design: Sadaaki Masuda and A. Scott Howe
Digital Drawing: Go Nishiyama, Shinichi Kasahara

Kiss + Cathcart, Architects

E-mail:gjkiss@aol.com

New York, New York 10038

Hamburg's Electrical Utility, Germany

Profile:

Kiss + Cathcart, Architects have been practicing in Lower Manhattan since 1984. They have focused on architecture which integrates economy, ecology and technology with design. In addition to residential and commercial work, K+C has specialized in industrial architecture, in computer technologies for design work, and in the integration of solar photovoltaics into the built environment.

Use of Digital Media:

In the context of developing new solar technologies for architectural applications, the firm has done basic research, industrial design, and solar simulations of various building-related systems. This has included extensive use of the computer for visual simulations including high quality renderings and animations. These are produced as a standard part of the design process in-house, not only for separate presentations.

Hardware and Software:

Apple Power Macintosh. MiniCAD, Strata StudioPro Blitz, and Adobe Photoshop.

Drawing Process/Image Technique:

The design was developed in MiniCAD (Macintosh) as a 3D model, from the earliest stages. For high quality renderings and animation, the model was imported in StudioPro by Strata.

Design Concept:

Hamburg's electrical utility, HEW, is one of the strongest supporters of solar energy in Germany. Ironically, their customer center, located in Hamburg's prestigious central shopping district, suffers from a cold and leaky facade. Besides inconveniencing the occupants, this building lacks the energy efficiency expected of a progressive utility company.

Kiss + Cathcart, Architects, proposed to solve the problem by draping a new photovoltaic glass skin over the existing building. This new skin not only protects against cold and moisture, it creates accessory space. By pulling away from the building in the center, the skin encloses a new wintergarden on the first floor while sheltering outdoor shopping and cafe space at street level. Most importantly, the PV facade generates electricity and heat, saving considerable amounts of energy throughout the year. The second skin approach has the added environmental benefit of eliminating the need for demolition and disposal of the existing facade.

The new facade is a complex curving shape comprised of over 1,200 glass and photovoltaic modules, most of which are different sizes and shapes. As one of the most complicated curtain walls ever constructed, this project intends to prove that photovoltaics can perform the most difficult architectural functions.

Credits:

Gregory Kiss
Kiss + Cathcart, Architects

KovertHawkins Architects

Web Site: www.koverthawkins.com
E-mail: john@koverthawkins.com

Jeffersonville, Indiana 47130

Southern Indiana Visitor's Center, Indiana

Profile:

KovertHawkins is a ten-person architectural firm located in southern Indiana, across the Ohio river from Louisville, Kentucky. The firm handles a variety of project types, with empahsis on educational, commercial, corporate and industrial work. The partners of the firm are Hal Kovert and John Hawkins. In addition to architectural and interior design work, the firm has provided digital and hand illustration work for a number of other design professionals.

Use of Digital Media:

Three dimensional computer models are used to study initial design concepts, and for refining designs. Wireframe, smooth shaded and quick raytraced renderings are used in-house. Client presentations are generally raytracing or radiosity renderings. Animations have been created for some projects, but high-resolution still renderings are the firm's preferred presentation method.

Hardware:

Macintosh Power PC's with Pentium PC Compatibility Cards. 160 MB RAM (Mac Side), 80 MB RAM (PC Side). HP755cm Color Plotter/Postscript Plotter. Fargo Primera Dye-Sublimation Printer. HP855 Color Printer. Epson Scanner.

Software:

Strata StudioPro, Autocad 14, Adobe Photoshop 4.0, Adobe PageMaker, Archicad 4.0.

Drawing Process / Image Technique:

Rendered to high resolution files in StudioPro, retouched and composited in Photoshop. Printed from PageMaker.

Concept:

Client desired a highly visible design to attract passing motorists. Building site was adjacent to client's office building, a restored historical structure.

Credits:

Partner in Charge: Hal Kovert, AIA
Project Manager: James Lake
Interiors: Elaine Simpson, NCIDQ
Rendering: John Hawkins, AIA

John Lumsden

E-mail: johnlumsden@yahoo.com
Web Site: www.hippo.cc

Los Angeles, California 90068

Water Treatment Lab and Administration Building, Long Beach, California
Mid-Rise #1, Seoul, Korea

▮ Profile:

John Lumsden received a Bachelor of Architecture from the University of Southern California and began working at DMJM in 1988. John completed several projects as project designer including the School of Social and Behavioral Sciences Building at Cal State University San Bernardino, and the Long Beach Water Treatment Plant Laboratory and Administration Building. As a founding member and partner of AJLA in 1994, John worked on a number of design competitions, and recently designed two mid-rise commercial office buildings.

▮ Use of Digital Media in the Office:

For John Lumsden the process of design does not change with the use of computers. What does change is the spontaneity of the design solution. As opposed to the conventional design process, the limitations of physical reality are not imposed in the abstract digital world of computers. The digital age desolves the structure of the traditional organization, freeing the designer from conventional notions of craft and teamwork.

▮ Hardware:

Networked workstations: Pentium 200 with 2 GB hard drive and 128 MB of RAM for rendering, and Pentium 120 with 128 MB RAM for modeling.

▮ Software:

AutoCAD, 3D Studio, Lightscape, Photoshop.

▮ Drawing Process/Digital Technique:

The initial development of solutions for problems and opportunities within the project were developed in traditional abstract conventions such as plan and section, but are formulated into an embryonic three dimensional solution within the first few days. The process of design begins with the analysis of the given parameters. Change and variation become a dynamic force in the total design process. As the design began to solidify, several computers were used to test lighting solutions and to produce high resolution images.

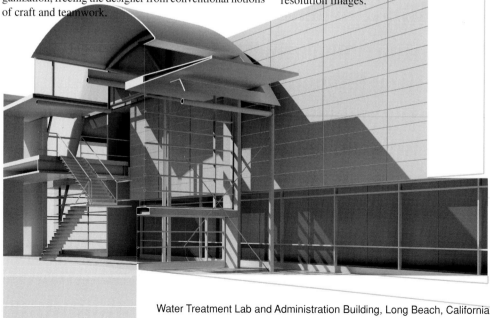

Water Treatment Lab and Administration Building, Long Beach, California

▌ Credits (Water Treatment Lab & Adm. Bldg.):

DMJM Architects/Engineers
Project Designer and Digital Images: John Lumsden
Design Principal: Tony Lumsden
Project A

▌ Credits (Mid-Rise #1, Seoul, Korea):

AJLA Architects
Project Architect and Digital Images: John Lumsden

145

Machado and Silvetti Associates, Inc.

Web Site: www.machado-silvetti.com
E-mail: Office@Machado-Silvetti.com
Boston, Massachusetts 02118

Sigma Sigma Commons Tower, University of Cincinnati, Cincinnati, Ohio
Sonic Drive-In Prototype

Profile:

Machado and Silvetti Associates, Inc. is an internationally recognized planning and design firm known for distinctive urban spaces and unique works of architecture. The office does not espouse any single architectural style, but strives to find that which is unique and important within a given project, and to express that urbanistically and architecturally. The firm's principals, Rodolfo Machado and Jorge Silvetti, have been in association since 1974. Both teach at the Harvard University Graduate School of Design, where Jorge Silvetti chairs the department of architecture. The firm's projects include additions to the Getty Villa in Malibu, California, a parking structure, dormitory and master plan for Princeton University, a new biomedical research campus plan for the University of California San Francisco, a dormitory for Rice University, a museum for the University of Utah, and Robert F. Wagner, Jr. Park in New York. Machado and Silvetti has received the First Award in Architecture, given by the American Academy of Arts and Letter, two AIA Honor Awards, eight *Progressive Architecture* Awards, as well as numerous design honors in Argentina, France, Germany, and Italy.

Machado and Silvetti's Use of Digital Media:

The computer has become an important tool throughout Machado and Silvetti's design and documentation process. Nearly every staff member in the office is now equipped with a dedicated workstation, and all current projects utilize CAD technology. Early two-dimensional floor plan diagrams are often drawn in illustration programs and later imported into CAD to be used as the basis for hard-lined drawings. Three-dimensional wire frame CAD drawings are used to create proper perspectives for hand colored renderings and also for aiding in the creation of basswood and chipboard models. More complex three-dimensional designs are developed using computer generated solid models rendered with realistic materials. All construction documents as well as most design development and urban planning drawings are created in CAD. These are then translated to create presentation and marketing graphics using various graphics programs. The firm also extensively employs photo-realistic rendered animations for presenta-

tions to clients and for selecting a material palette. Finally all phases of design can be imported to an Internet file format for inclusion on the company web site, Intranet site, and Extranet sites.

Hardware:

Platform: IBM-compatible personal computers with Pentium II processors and Power Macintosh computers with G3 processors.
Input Devices: color flatbed scanner, large-format B&W scanner.
Output Devices: B&W laser printers, B&W and color large-format plotters, color ink-jet printer.
Storage: Syquest, Zip, and Jaz drives, CD-ROM writer.

Software:

Microsoft Windows NT4, MS Exchange 5, MS Office 97, MS Internet Explorer 4, Adobe PageMaker 6.5, Adobe Photoshop 5, Adobe Illustrator 7, Adobe Acrobat 3, Autodesk AutoCAD Release 14, and Autodesk 3D StudioMAX 2.

Drawing Process / Image Technique:

Rough computer models for the Sigma Sigma Commons Tower and the Sonic Drive-In Restaurant were created with the three-dimensional modeling component of AutoCAD. These rough models were then imported into 3D Studio for rendering and animating. Due to the small size of the tower, it was possible to study many options for the design of the lantern at top. Final renderings were printed in house on an HP 750C printer and out-of-house as Iris prints. For Sonic, many texture maps of the graphic elements were delivered electronically by the client, Lippincott & Margulies, as Tiff files for insertion into the final model. After lights, texture maps, cameras, and entourage were added, renderings were done to fine-tune the images before final renderings and animation. Animation files were produced in-house, but the actual rendering of the animations and subsequent transfer to videotape were completed by an out-of-house service.

**Sigma Sigma Commons Tower,
University of Cincinnati, Cincinnati, Ohio**

▌ Concept:

A new master plan commissioned by the University of Cincinnati replaces an existing 500-car parking lot with a large commons at the center of the undergraduate campus.

The Sigma Sigma Commons Tower is designed to act as a landmark, a gathering point, and an icon for this new space. The design stacks varied elements that symbolize the University and donor, Sigma Sigma Fraternity. These are portrayed in layers of various materials: concrete, wood, metal, precast concrete, and stainless steel. At night, the perforated lantern at top can be lit from below, and the color of light can change according to campus events.

Credits (Sigma Sigma Commons Tower):

Machado and Silvetti Associates, Inc.
Jorge Silvetti (Partner-in-Charge) with Rodolfo Machado, Elizabeth Gibb (Project Architect), Nader Tehrani and Andrew Ku (Design Assistants), Ben Karty (Computer Modeling).

Sonic Drive-In Prototype

Concept:

This fast food drive-in prototype for Sonic Restaurants was developed with Lippincott & Margulies, a corporate identity firm. The prototype's design seeks a consistent and singular image that is clearly legible and distinct from a passing car. The goal has been to combine all of the disparate elements of a drive-in (canopies, the kitchen building, patio areas, car stalls, and columns) into an integrated design. By reducing visual clutter, the image of the Sonic Restaurant brand can stand out more clearly. The design taps into nostalgic feelings for the golden age of drive-in restaurants, an era that was infused with aerodynamic imagery that connotes speed and directionality (qualities that

Sonic Drive-In Prototype

are legible from an automobile). As a strong sculptural object, the prototype distinguishes itself within the context of the highway strip.

▌ Credits (Sonic Drive-In Prototype):

Machado and Silvetti Associates, Inc.
Rodolfo Machado (Partner-in-Charge) with Jorge Silvetti, Timothy Love (Project Director), Nader Tehrani and Rusty Walker (Design Team), David Lee and Ben Karty (Computer Modeling).

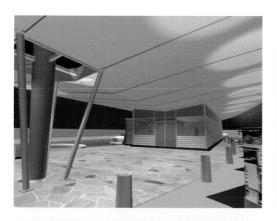

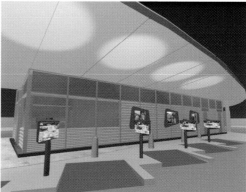

Morphosis

E-mail: Morphosis@earthlink.com

Santa Monica, California 90404

ASE Design Center, Shih-chic, Taipei, Taiwan
Hypothenkenbank, Klagenfurt, Austria

Profile:

'Morphosis' was founded with the objective of developing unique projects which focus on the multiple needs predicated by the project brief, site, and client. "We are interested in challenging ourselves with a variety of design problems, and have resisted becoming specialized in any particular building type....We are particularly interested in pursuing work for those clients who have a truly longterm vision regarding the value of good architecture." The firm's personnel resources are comprised of an experienced group of 20+ professionals and additional support staff directed by principal Thom Mayne.

Morphosis' practice is broadly diversified. Since their founding twenty years ago, they have successfully completed over 65 projects, and have been consistently recognized by the peers as cutting edge innovators. Morphosis has been the recipient of 17 Progressive Architecture Awards and 19 AIA Awards since 1974. Morphosis has been the subject of fifteen monographs and innumerable articles in publications around the world.

Use of Digital Media:

"Computers arrived to our studio without deification. We made no attempt to make our work look digital - quite the opposite. The inherent workings of the computer were very compatible and transitional to the operational methods we utilized in the first twenty years: reiteration, layering, methods of relation or connectedness...... Morphosis is currently producing all of our projects with computer technology. Rather than compromise either modeling, drafting or rendering by subscribing wholly to one all-encompassing software package, our method diversifies task-specific programs. We operate primarily on the Macintosh platform, utilizing Form •Z by Autodes-sys and Powerdraw by Engineered Software for the majority of our CADD documents. The initial design is created and modified with the use of three dimensional software and high-end rendering programs (Form•Z, Electric Image, Studio Pro, etc.) A continual refinement of the 3D model both informs the design and brings another level of precision and coherence to the project. At a certain point in the design devel-

150

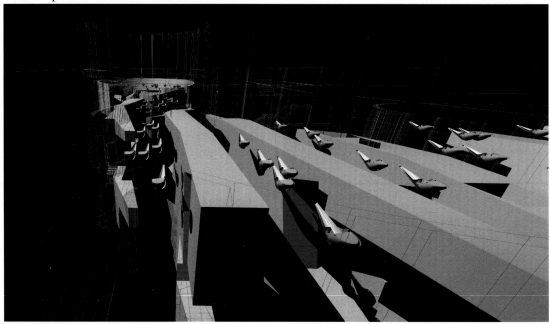

opment, 2D, "DXF" files are exported out of Form•Z and brought into Powerdraw for manipulation of line weight, notes, and formatting. We use 3D Studio to create photo-real images (snapshots really) and to render objects selectively. Graphic presentations are developed primarily using Adobe Photoshop and QuarkXPress."

Hardware and Software:

Power Macintosh. Form •Z for 3D modeling; 3D Max and Electric Image for rendering.

Drawing Process/Digital Technique:

Form•Z was used primarily to model and manipulate the object. Once the bulk of the 3D modeling was done, the model was exported into 3D Max and Electric Image to be rendered and further explored.

Design Concept:

ASE Design Center: The Center is a gathering place for the Taiwanese Design community and visitors to the Com-

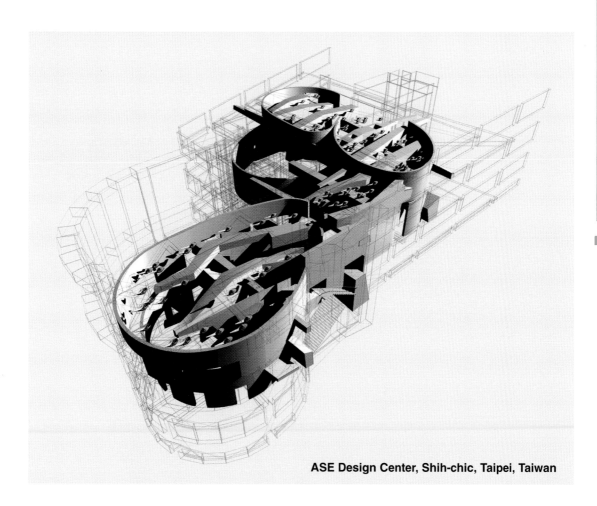

ASE Design Center, Shih-chic, Taipei, Taiwan

plex. The Visitor Center frees itself from the constraints of the existing complex. Two contrary architectural impositions are implemented. The two interact to create a conceptual abstract framework from which a new vocabulary is derived. Radius walls of plate steel are used to establish and accommodate the distinct programmatic functions of the Visitor Center. The shells define the restaurant, cafe, lecture hall, and various places of exhibition. The second device is a response of the existing, seemingly non-ordered nature of the structural grid. A system of angular, folded volumes house a veritable forest of large random columns. From these forms a 3 dimensional volumetric matrix is mapped out. All points of intersections, folds and facets are translated into a coordinate system.

The pieces transform the static and irregular columns to fleeting and ephemeral vectors. The pieces denote energy and are informed by the functions contained within-, lighting, heating ventilation and air conditioning. Constructed of a lightweight steel frame, and clad in a skin of white, an ideal armature for exhibition is provided, a backdrop for the unusual and the unexpected. The two systems combine to create an organizing whole. The strength and permanence of the rusted steel walls is juxtaposed to the movement and dynamism of the white shards. Opposing forces are neutralized as they become one. Resolution is found as the concurrent forces coexist in harmonious tension.

Credits: Morphosis

Hypothenkenbank, Klagenfurt, Austria

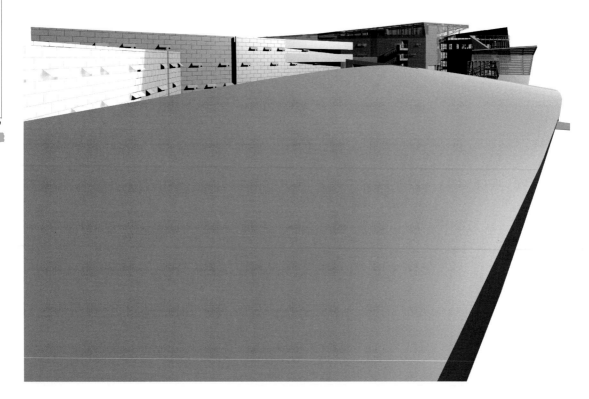

▌ Design Concept:

Kartner Landes-und Hypothenkenbank AG: The urban strategy for the new Karntner Landes-und Hypothenkenbank focuses on three major ideas: The creation of a large roof structure which serves to form a cohesiveness and scale relationship to the new development, the new Hypobank building which emerges from the development and manifests itself as an important cultural civic building, and the integration of the surrounding housing with the site.

The proposal attempts to integrate the low density of the suburban context to the north and east with a more densely urban structure to the south along Volkermarkter Strabe. The roof is a conceptual "landscape", a fragment of the rural topography reinterpreted as open space which will become increasingly evident as future growth resituates this site within the urban context in contrast to its current edge relationship.

The building is lifted above ground at the corner of Vokermarkter Strabe and Kudlichgasse to form a large covered public space leading visitors to the bank lobby event center. The ceiling of the bank is glazed with a view to the courtyard above. Elevators and stairs service the building from the P-1 levels to the fourth floor creating lobbies at each floor with views to the court below. Office departments are organized by floor according to program requirements. Building materials of glass, perforated metal and metal panels articulate the different elements of the building and give varied character to each department, while volumes of the building terminates at the corner to form a synbolic entry into the new development.

Credits: Morphosis

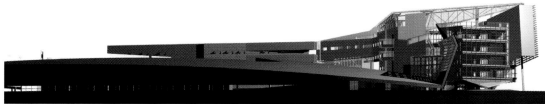

Hypothenkenbank, Klagenfurt, Austria

Eric Owen Moss Architects

Web Site: ericowenmoss@ juno.com/

Culver City, California 90232

Pittard Sullivan Office Building, Culver City, California

Profile:

Eric Owen Moss opened his office in 1973 in Angeles. Moss was educated at Berkeley and Harvard. He has recently held professorial chairs at Yale, Harvard, and appointments in Copenhagen and Vienna, in addition to Sci-Arc, where he began teaching in 1973 and is currently on the Board of Directors. His work has recently been exhibited in Duren, Germany; Barcelona, Spain; Tokyo, Japan; Lisbon, Portugal; Copenhagen, Denmark; and he was one of the four American architects invited to represent the U.S.A. at the 1996 Venice Biennale. A second Rizzoli monograph - *ERIC OWEN MOSS: BUILDINGS AND PROJECTS 2* was published in 1995, along with *THE BOX*, published by Princeton Architectural Press in 1996, and *THE LAWSON/WESTEN HOUSE* published by Phaidon Press in 1994. Upcoming books include *GNOSTIC ARCHITECTURE*, a statement/manifesto of Moss' theory of design, to be published by Monacelli Press in 1998; *PS* and *10 YEARS AND THE NEW CITY* to be published by Images Press also in 1998. Current projects include work in Vienna, Spain, France, New York, Los Angeles, and Culver City. Moss is the recipient of 34 design awards from Progressive Architecture and the American Institute of Architecture and is a fellow of the American Institute of Architecture.

Eric Owen Moss's Use of Digital Media:

Digital media has become an integral part of the design and representation in a variety of ways from initial design conception phases to final presentation.

In its initial phase, three-dimensional computer models allow for quick study of formal/organizational structures easily translatable to and from physical models. As the project progresses, computer models are precisely reworked and reconstructed in conjunction with physical models as exact sizes and materials are known. This allows tight control of complex form and quick access to topological and formal information that was previously done by hand using descriptive geometry techniques. When modeling complex forms, physical models are occasion-

ally laser-scanned and then reworked in the computer to deal tolerances and exact locations. Building detailed computer models has given insight into the process and type of construction through the inherent structures of representing form in the computer. Computer models are directly linked to and are the basis for two-dimensional representation both in the creation of construction documents and presentations. When a building is in construction, the computer model is used to check shop drawings and dimensions in the field.

Computer models also become a basis for understanding and dissecting the building designs and their interrelationships through renderings and sometimes animations. These representations are done in a descriptive rather than a realistic way and show how a building works as opposed to how it looks. Once built, photographic representations of the buildings are occasionally digitally stitched or mixed with renderings to give views/ photos unattainable through traditional photo techniques.

Hardware:

Pentium processor based IBM Personal Computer with 64 MB min RAM.

Software:

AutoCAD, 3D Studio and Rhino for modeling. 3D Studio, Photoshop, for rendering and post production.

Drawing Process/Digital Technique:

The images in this book show a variety of digital imaging from the Pittard Sullivan Building. These images are used here to illustrate the variety and types of imaging in order to represent the building both before and after construction. The main purpose of the computer models used was for understanding the building and particularly the lobby for drawings and construction.

154

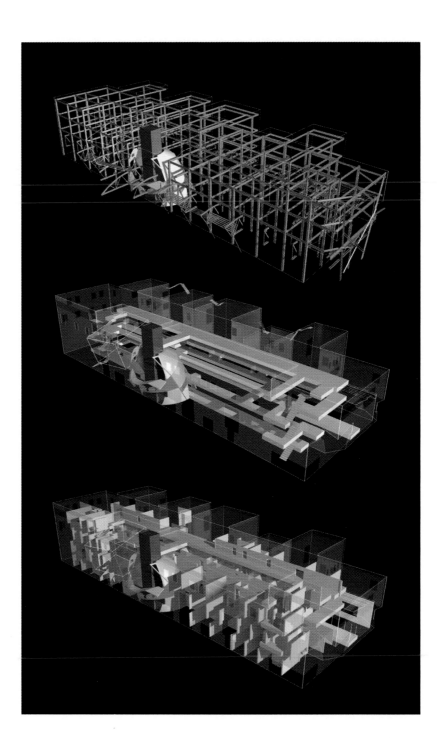

Drawing Process / Image Technique:

The three views of Pittard Sullivan Office Building show different systems of building in an attempt to show how this complex building is assembled in terms of structure, circulation, and program division. This building was modeled, then rendered using transparencies to see through the building.

155

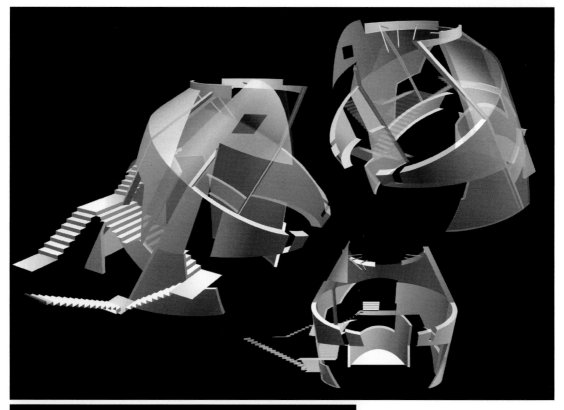

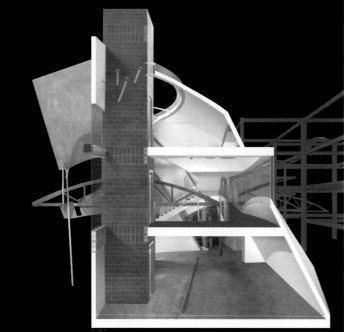

Drawing Process / Image Technique:

Above: The three views of only the lobby were rendered transparently in order to understand them simultaneously as external form and internal space. The images were modeled with AutoCAD 12, rendered in 3D Studio and laid out and touched up in Photoshop.

Left: The photo section of PS Lobby is a section created by photographing the space and the stitching the photos on top of a rendered computer model used as a guide. This gives a reading of the lobby unattainable through traditional media.

Design Concept:

Pittard Sullivan Office Building: The building recollects forward, acknowledging its past and the history of the area, while moving decisively forward to create the landmark headquarters for a digital motion picture graphic design company. The ancillary buildings were removed from the site except for a single brick wall and the double bow string truss system. A four story steel frame of wide flange beams and tube columns were built over the bow strings, which now extend beyond the south wall and are exposed. A sequence of parallel walls follows the frames that follow the trusses; the south wall at the parking/building perimeter, a pair that enclose the double loaded corridor, and a third that closes the office block. The building is enlarged by hooking four office blocks to the north wall.

Credits:

Eric Owen Moss Architects
Digital Image: Paul Groh

Drawing Process / Image Technique:

The photomontage is digitally stitched together to unfold a space that is very difficult to photograph. This was done by photographing the space from a single vantage and then carefully rearranging and stitching the images in Photoshop.

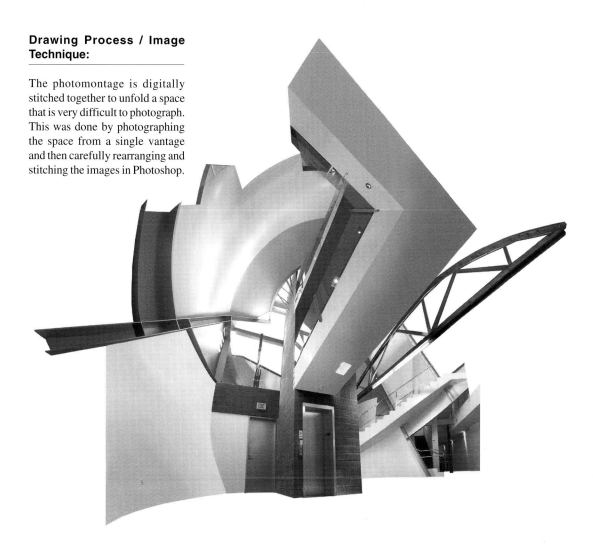

NBBJ

Web Site: www.nbbj.com
E-mail: website@nbbj.com

Seattle, Washington • Columbus, Ohio • Los Angeles, California • New York, New York • San Francisco, California • Research Triangle Park, North Carolina •Tokyo • Taipei • Oslo

Profile:

NBBJ is the world's fifth largest architecture firm with a staff of 800 and projects throughout North America, South America, Central Asia, and Europe. Although the firm practices in twenty-one studios, spread among six U.S. offices, it is not diffused or disconnected. NBBJ has a strong, coherent identity and mission, but gives its staff extraordinary autonomy and freedom. The firm's leadership is rigorously design focused and architecturally visionary; however, it is as strongly committed to serving its clients and society as it is to producing exceptional design. NBBJ's expertise spans a broad range of design practices. No building or interior designed by NBBJ reflects a single, firm-defining style, but every project is informed by the same set of complex, deeply held principles. There are few, if any, building types the firm has not created. To each project, NBBJ studios bring a balance of design, technology, process, and communication. The design leaders of these individual studios not only lead the efforts within their own groups but also provide collaborative design critique across all the firm's studios.

NBBJ's Use of Digital Media:

NBBJ is pioneering how architects explore, inform, and document the design process for clients and contractors/builders around the world. One unique process that began two years ago and is now starting to bear fruit on several of the firm's projects, is the use of 3-dimensional electronic models of the built environment coupled with that of physical model explorations. However it is the use of 3D software packages that have increased NBBJ's ability to explore the architect and client design vision(s) in a faster and more fluid manner. Computer technology has allowed the firm to open a world of 3-dimensional plasticity, richness, and complexity, which just a few years ago, the human mind's eye could only fathom.

NBBJ is leading the architecture community in visualization by incorporating 3D technology throughout the entire design process of exploration, documentation, and implementation. With Silicon Graphics hardware, Alias/wavefront 3D visualization software, and MicroStation Trimforma 3D documentation software, the firm is better able to explore the forms, spaces, and connections in a facile real-time mode and to make intelligent and efficient decisions. For example, computer studies in light, materiality, and animation give the design team(s) an additional fourth dimension of time. This process allows the archi-

tects to work more closely with the client, exploring design solution(s) evident from the virtual environment. Realistic renderings (that without this technology routinely takes several days to complete) show shadow and light studies of sun angles and paths to provide added depth and information. The capability to explore material options in this format with the client also expedites the decision making process.

Exploration with 3D technology is not just limited to 3D electronic data. NBBJ is also revolutionizing the conventional physical tool sets used by architects. For further design studies, design team(s) extract 3D electronic data from the computer and use this data on various manufacturing tools to build 3D physical models that are more tactile and can physically relate the objects' scale. Whether it is laser cutting plexi-glass and wood or the use of SLA (Stereo-Lithography) polymer resins to create a physical model, the design team(s) now have an increasing palette and resourceful tool combinations. Consequently, the two design methods (virtual and physical) complement and inform each other throughout the design process.

Documentation of the 3D electronic data for use by the contractor/builder is a critical step in NBBJ's design process. It is this step that again distinguishes NBBJ from many other architects. Through the use of isometric and axonometric drawings document readers are actually shown scalable objects and design elements. Slicing sections through 3D data for 2D documentation help to eliminate future coordination problems and inform the design team(s) of vital decisions that, when made early and correctly can increase project efficiency. NBBJ implements the 3D electronic data directly from Alias/wavefront software and transfers this information to the contractor/builder for the construction of full-scale parts for the final building design. This use of electronic data for manufacturing columns and moldings as well as analyzing complex curtain walls and their shapes directly with contractors further increases project efficiency.

Hardware and Software (for all images):

Hardware: Networked Silicon Graphics 02's, 256 MB RAM, 10GB Hard Drive.

Software: Alias, Wavefront Designer, Form•Z Renderzone, 3D Studio Max, MicroStation, Photoshop.

Kwun Tong Town Centre, Hong Kong

Credits:

Partner-in-Charge: James O. Jonassen
Principal-in-Charge: Dorman D. Anderson
Design Principal: Peter Pran
Project Designers:
Joey Myers and Jonathan Ward
Technical Designer: Duncan J. Griffin
Model Designer: Alexander Vassiliadis
Graphic Designers: Susan Dewey, Paul
Gillis, and Jordan Hukee
Video Design/Production: Joe Rettenmaier

Design Concept:

Kwun Tong Town Centre is designed to create the heart of a city within the larger Hong Kong metropolitan area. It possesses the inherent spontaneity and power recognizable worldwide as a landmark urban event. Based on several key urban and architectural design goals, the project is integrated with an intuitive and emotional response to the site. Serendipitous possibilities exist for linking the various program pieces into a place where people want to live, shop, work and play. Inherent to the scheme is the juxtaposition of rational modern movement systems (buses, cars, and trains) with pedestrian traffic flow. A people-mover carries commuters from the MTR station into a magnificent interior atrium that defines the project's core and converges pedestrian activities.

Telenor Headquarters, Fornebu, Oslo, Norway

Design Concept:

This magnificent and dynamic building complex for 6,000 Telenor staff (workplace and meeting rooms being the dominant features) is built along a former international airport runway. As architecture and profile, Telenor Headquarters will stand out as exciting, organic, friendly, and dignified. Its form is new and complex, setting precedence as visionary architecture for the next century and welcoming visitors and staff from many angles and points: the air, ground, and nearby Oslofjord. The design grows out its former airport and waterfront location, placed in low integration with the site and surrounding landscape. Two curved major circulation boulevards define the main entry while the central exterior space links to the major "offices-of-the-future" wings creating a spectacular movement throughout the complex itself and towards the Oslofjord. In partnership HUS Sivilarkitekter MNAL and PKA.

Credits:

Partner-in-Charge: Scott Wyatt

Design Principal: Peter Pran

Project Manger: Jim Waymire

Lead Senior Designers:
Joey Myers and Joseph T. Herrin

Senior Designers:
Jonathan Ward and Jin Ah Park

Designers:
Mike Mora, Frederick Norman, Suzanne Zahr, Curtis Wagner, Kay Compton, and Case Creal

Model Designer:
Alexander Vassiliadis

Graphic Designers:
Susan Dewey and Jordan Hukee

Reebok World Headquarters Canton, Massachusetts

Design Concept:

The design of Reebok's new world headquarters mirrors the shoe and fitness company's own design process and is driven by the shared vision of achieving high level performance. The architectural function and expression synthesize sporting activities with Reebok's products and people. Each component takes on multiple associations, connections, and viewing, as well as the ability to alter and grow. Spaces and forms are conveyed in a series of disparate parts: product design, marketing and sales, administration, community, fitness, and presentation. The building form represents Reebok's integrity achieved through the provocative balance of the architecture of movement combined with the aesthetic of sincere and honest materials.

Credits:

Partner-in-Charge: Scott Wyatt
Partner-in-Charge of Design: Richard G. Buckley

Design Principal: Steven McConnell
Project Principal: K. Robert Swartz
Project Designer: Jonathan Ward
Lead Interior Designer: Chris Larson
Project Architect: Gary Schaefer
Senior Technical Designer: Nick Charles
Technical Designer: Andrew Bromberg
Designers: Dave Burger, Daniel Cockrell, Case Creal, Yumiko Fujimori, Cory Harris, Nick Hendrickson, Shiki Huangyutitham, Steve Joo, Michael Kreis, John Millard, Joey Myers, Terrance O'Neil, Jin Ah Park, Sarah Pelone, Carsten Stinn, Alan Young
Cost Estimators: Jay F. Halleran and Derek Ryan
Model Designer: Alexander Vassiliadis
Video Design/Production: Joe Rettenmaier
Graphic Designers: Susan Dewey, Diane Anderson, Roddy Grant, Jordan Hukee, and Leo Raymundo

LG Twins Seoul Dome, Seoul, South Korea

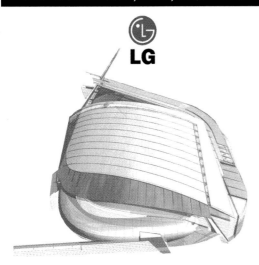

Design Concept:

A unified whole is the central concept for the LG Twins Seoul Dome, a multi-purpose, all-weather stadium in conjunction with a two million square foot retail and entertainment center. The stadium will serve as an international symbol of Seoul and its inviting new urban culture. Each program element occupies a distinctive building mass. These elements are carved, bent, and interwoven to create a dynamic but unified and indivisible whole. The strong physical relationships between the building masses create intended and unexpected tensions that give the project a pulsating energy. The dynamic character, however, is controlled by structural and architectural economies, and visually resolved and balanced in its design. The 43,000-seat Seoul Dome will become the permanent home for the LG Twins Baseball Team and reflect the corporate image of the LG Group. The stadium is also slated to host the 2002 World Cup Soccer Games.

Credits:

NBBJ Sports & Entertainment
Principal-in-Charge:
Michael Hallmark

Design Principals:
Dan Meis and Peter Pran

Project Principal: Jim Waymire

Project Manager: Ignatius Chau

Lead Technical Designer:
Michael Hootman

Lead Designers:
Joey Myers and Jonathan Ward

Designers: Mike Amaya,
Jonathan Emmett, Peter Fergin,
Greg Lombardi, Greg Lyon,
Salvador Hidalgo, Seung Lee,
Bryan Tessner, John Lodge, and
Keith Collins

Graphic Designers: Diane
Anderson and Brent Whiting

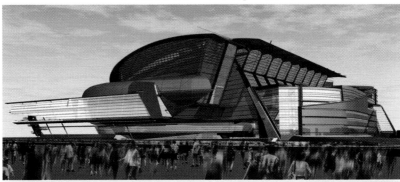

■ Digital Architecture

Paul Brown Stadium, Cincinnati, Ohio

Design Concept:

Cincinnati's new 67,000-seat NFL stadium breaks with tradition and eliminates corner seating that allows for views right through the megastructure. The architectural language expresses the energy of the game. The building is in motion. Horizontal lines guide the eye around the facility. Concrete skins peel to reveal inner layers of metal and glass that define and display the circulation ramps and interior spaces. The sleek inside is equipped with 2 massive club lounges and 112 luxury suites. The design culminates in a roof structure that makes a complex sweep across the sky ending in a 65-foot cantilever that thrusts past the upper deck. The design, a recipient of an American Architecture Award, invites the entire city to engage in the spectacle.

163

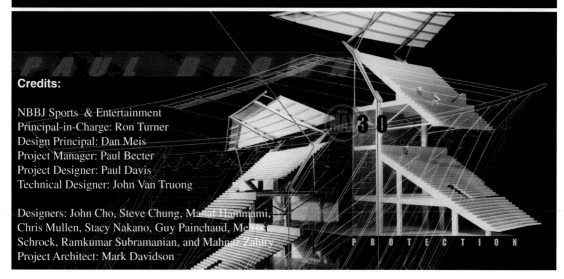

Credits:

NBBJ Sports & Entertainment
Principal-in-Charge: Ron Turner
Design Principal: Dan Meis
Project Manager: Paul Becter
Project Designer: Paul Davis
Technical Designer: John Van Truong

Designers: John Cho, Steve Chung, Manaf Hammami, Chris Mullen, Stacy Nakano, Guy Painchaud, Melissa Schrock, Ramkumar Subramanian, and Mahnaz Zahiry
Project Architect: Mark Davidson

Nelson Design

Web Site: www.members.aol.com/Nelsondsgn
E-mail: Nelsondsgn@aol.com

Riverside, Illinois 60546

Alternate Design for the Arts Club of Chicago, Chicago, Illinois

Profile:

Nelson Design offers award-winning illustration, design and visualization services to architects and interior designers. Rendering projects range from virtual website interiors to kiosks to office buildings to community master plans. Through it all, the emphasis is on the timeless goal of communicating form and emotion through light and shadow.

Use of Digital Media:

Digital media are used for all activities in the office, from preliminary design sketches through detailed renderings. More and more projects are conducted without physical client contact, making geographic distance meaningless. In one project, a temporary web site was set up so that everyone involved could see updates in their browser.

Above all, technology is adapted to the needs of each client

Hardware:

Intel Petium Processors 160 & 200MHz, Matrox Millenium 8MB RAM video card, Viewsonic 17PS monitors, Western Digital Caviar storage drive, Quantum Viking SCSI3 hard drive, HP Scanjet 5 scanner, HP Deskjet 1000 color printer, Iomega 100MB Zip and 1 GB Jaz drive.

Software:

Windows NT 4.0, AutoCAD for Windows, AccuRender Raytracer, Corel Photo-Paint, People for People, Adobe Premier, Lightscape.

▌ Drawing Process / Image Technique:

The building was designed and modeled in AutoCAD. AccuRender was used to create and assign materials, to set the lighting, and to raytrace the final image. The ripples, carpet and tree were procedural processes. The people and other entourage were 3D meshes. Photo-Paint was used sparingly to touch up the contrast and to smooth a few rough edges.

▌ Concept:

A proposed alternative to the "correct" but bland design for the new Arts Club of Chicago. Dynamic form and strong color are borrowed from the Miesian tradition, as well as references to contemporary visual artists (in this case Claes Oldenberg/Coosje van Bruggen's sculpture, and painter Fern Valfer's abstract, space-defining curves). The building is a repository for Art, and an art object designed from the inside out.

165

▌ Credits:

Design, Modeling,
and Illustration:
Mark S. C. Nelson, AIA.

Cesar Pelli & Associates

Web Site: www.cesar-pelli.com

New Haven, Connecticut 06510

National Museum of Contemporary Art, Osaka, Japan
International Finance Center, Hong Kong

▌ Profile:

Cesar Pelli & Associates is a full service architectural firm with substantial credentials and experience. The firm's first commission in 1977 was the Museum of Modern Art Expansion and Renovation in New York City. Subsequent projects have continued a consistent history of high quality built work of increasing variety. Clients, programs, sites and budgets are diverse, enabling Cesar Pelli & Associates to gain expertise in a broad array of building types. The firm has worked with corporate, government and private clients to design major public spaces, museums, airports, laboratories, performing arts centers, academic buildings, hotels, office and residential towers and mixed-use projects.

The American Institute of Architects (AIA) awarded Cesar Pelli the 1995 Gold Medal, which recognizes a lifetime of distinguished achievement and outstanding contributions. Additionally, the AIA awarded Cesar Pelli & Associates its 1989 Firm Award in recognition of over a decade of standard-setting work in architectural design; Cesar Pelli has received over 100 awards for design excellence.

▌ Use of Digital Media:

Cesar Pelli & Associates has over 13 years of experience using computers in its design process. Starting in 1986 with 4 personal computers, the firm's accumulative knowledge in CADD, 3D computer modeling, photo-realistic ren-

National Museum of Contemporary Art, Osaka, Japan

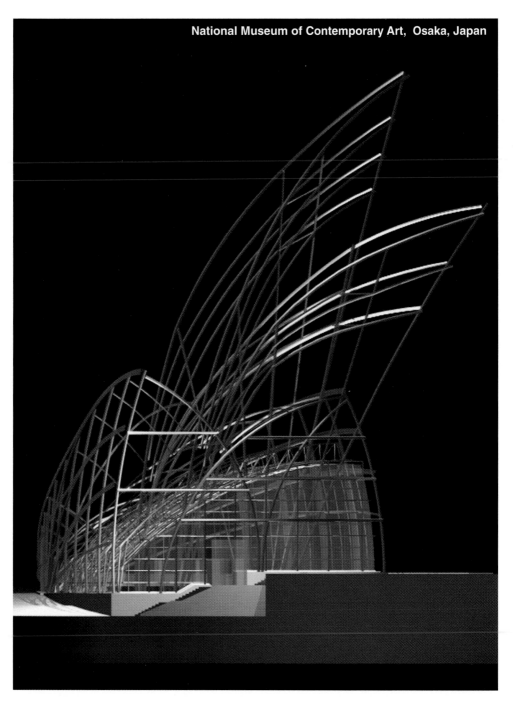

National Museum of Contemporary Art, Osaka, Japan

dering and animation has steadily grown to over 50 work-stations in the design studio. Without relying on specialized operators or a CADD department, over 90% of the design staff are trained to fully utilize the power and precision of the computer in the creative process. Since 1990, all projects executed in the office, including all of it's recent large scale projects, have been designed and documented with the aid of the computer.

"In our design process, we have focused on the use of the computer in the early phases of the design. We use it to better convey our design intentions with realistic renderings as well as to assist in site planning, model making and program and systems analyses. The computer is especially well suited for rapid examination of alternatives once the conceptual design has been established. In addition to the use of CAD as our primary application, we utilize a great variety of the digital media for the purposes of presentation and visualization."

Hardware:

Platform: Intel processor-based PC computers.
Input Devices: 35mm slide scanner, Flatbed opaque scanner, Digital cameras, Video capture device, Digitizers.
Output Devices: B&W large format plotters, B&W laser printers, Color large format plotters, Color ink-jet printers, Color dye sublimation printer.
Storage: Syquest 200MB removable cartridge drive, Iomega Zip drive, Iomega Jaz drive, CD-ROM reader and writer.

Software:

Microsoft Windows 95 & 98 for Operating Systems, Autocad r14 w/ Accurender 3, M-Color 4.02 for CAD, 3D Studios for 3D, Lightscape 2.0 for Rendering, Photoshop 5.0, Paintshop Pro 4.1 for image manipulation, Illustrator 7.0 for Illustration, Quark Xpress 4.0 for Desktop Publishing, Microsoft Office Suite and Filemaker Pro for Office Management.

Drawing Process/ Imaging Technique:

"Three sources contribute to the original material produced in our office. The origins can be computer drawings, digital photographs of physical models or scanned files of hand illustrations. The processes and the techniques adopted for any particular project depends on the both the source of the original and the ultimate product."

The majority of the drawings in the office originate in

Autocad. For presentation purposes, color is often added to the plans, sections and elevations, printed with large format plotters and mounted on boards. 3D computer models can originate either in Autocad or 3D Studios and are used for various visualization purposes. Quick studies can be done convincingly within Autocad using Accurender. More elaborate models are rendered in 3D Studios and careful lighting studies are carried out with the use of radiosity function in Lightscape. Full animations are carried out in 3D Studios and transferred to video with the assistance of outside services.

"Our process still uses physical models as the primary means of design. The digital camera helps us document and share our design process with our clients. Often, in the early phases of design, the digital images can be very useful for working reviews by adding hand rendering on top of color prints of model images. We continue to rely heavily on a small group of individuals who possess the hand and eye to create hand renderings in the traditions of architectural drawings. The current technology however, offers us the flexibility to enhance the presentation of the artwork in terms of the size and tonality. The renderings are often done very quickly in a convenient size, then scanned and printed to much larger images."

National Museum of Contemporary Art Osaka, Japan

Adjacent to the existing Science Museum on the island of Nakano, the Museum will be distributed on three levels below grade. The first level is the public free zone, followed by two levels of temporary and permanent gallery space. The design of the lightweight stainless steel structure of the museum entrance has been conceived as a sculptural form on an important view corridor within the city.

International Finance Centre, Hong Kong

The new International Finance Centre reflects the importance of Hong Kong as a world financial center and will be an integral part of the new air terminal station, which offers express service to the new Chek Lap Kok Airport. Phase One includes a 420-meter tall northeast office tower of approximately 181,000 square meter (sqm); a 210-meter tall southwest office tower of 73,000 sqm; and, a four-story retail podium of 50,000 sqm with a public roof garden.

▌ Credits:

Cesar Pelli & Associates Inc. Architects
New Haven Connecticut
Principals: Cesar Pelli FAIA, Fred W Clarke FAIA, and Rafael Pelli AIA
Digital Drawing (Museum of Contemporary Art, Osaka): G. Bakerman

International Finance Centre, Hong Kong

169

Pentagram Architecture

E-mail: architecture@pentagram.com
Web Site: www.pentagram.com

New York, New York 10010

Museum of Science and Industry, Chicago, Illinois, "Genetics: Decoding Life"

Profile:

Pentagram is an international design consultancy founded in London in 1972. It was originally founded by five partners: an architect, a product designer and three graphic designers. Gradually, the firm added more partners and expanded to New York in 1978, San Francisco in 1986, and Austin, Texas in 1995. There are now 14 partners and a total support staff of 140 who handle projects for national and international clients.

Architecture has been part of Pentagram's multi-disciplinary practice from the beginning of the partnership. Pentagram's London office has been involved in a variety of building and restoration projects in the UK and Europe, from analyzing the use and development of historical and cultural sites to creating exciting new commercial and residential environments. In the US, Pentagram has been involved in similar work including new restaurants, exhibitions, houses, retail space, and public monuments.

Pentagram's organization assures the best of both worlds for its clients: like a small private firm, each partner has direct and intimate involvement with the design work and with his or her clients; like a large international firm, the group maintains a sophisticated support structure and a large network of resources.

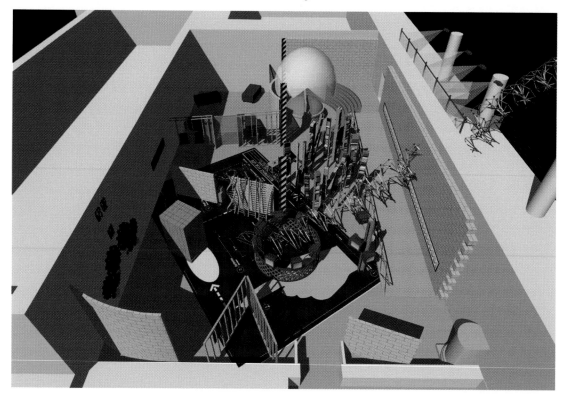

Pentagram's Use of Digital Media:

As a company, Pentagram is uniquely structured to provide not only the strong concepts needed for effective design solutions, but also optimum service in implementing these ideas. Pentagram is fully computerized (CAD) and regularly draws upon the expertise of the best professionals in related fields. Pentagram uses Microstation to generate all of it's two-dimensional drawing. From this 2-D drawing a three-dimensional representation is rendered using Form•Z.

Hardware and Software:

The Hardware used for all of the projects was a Power Macintosh 8500/150.

The Software used for all of the projects was Form•Z and Microstation.

Museum of Science and Industry, Chicago, Illinois "Genetics: Decoding Life" exhibit design

Design Concept:

"Genetics: Decoding life" is an exhibition planned to open in 1999 at the Museum of Science and Industry in Chicago. An investigation into DNA, the exhibit employs the metaphor that DNA, like blueprints, are instructions for life. Exposed walls and ceiling, steel scaffolding, and a gigantic blueprint on the floor create the construction site theme.

Credits:

Partner: James Biber
Associate: Michael Zweck-Bronner
Design Team: James Cleary, Tonya Van Cott, Karen Mustafellos, Ivan Arenas, Michael Wills

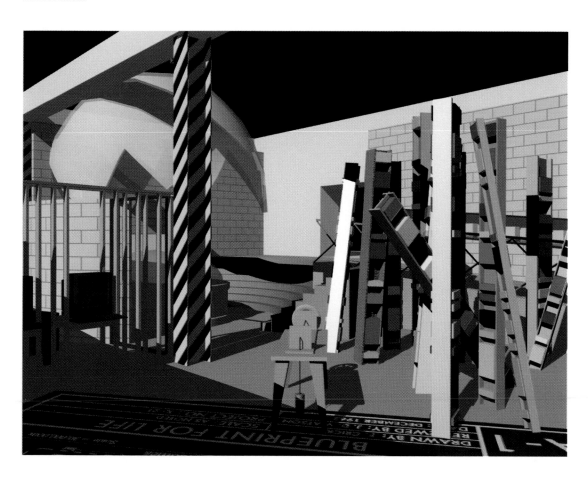

Perkins & Will

Web Site: www.perkinswill.com

Atlanta, Charlotte, Chicago, Los Angeles, Miami, Minneapolis, New York

Suburban Mixed-Use Office and Manufacturing Facility. Elgin, Illinois
Lynn Classical High School, Lynn, Massachusetts
Cyber Café, Illinois Institute of Technology, Institute of Design
LG Bundang R&D Complex, Seoul, Korea

Profile:

Perkins & Will, founded in 1935, first gained national recognition as a pioneer in American progressive school design. Today the firm's diversified international practice has received numerous design awards, and has expanded to also include the design of corporate and mixed-use developments, healthcare facilities, research and development facilities, hotels and conference centers, airports, and interior architecture. The firm's approach and commitment to high quality, progressive design is exemplified in this statement from Ralph Johnson: "We believe that architecture is a social art, which is the synthesis of site, climate and program. Our buildings are a unique response to a set of specific circumstances developed through a team process of consensus building. We are offering this process, as opposed to a preconceived product, and are striving for an architecture that is adaptive and responsive to the specific needs of our clients."

Perkins & Wills' Use of Digital Media:

Perkins & Will operates as a single firm with regional offices which share expertise. Networked communication in the form of a firm-wide Intranet, which includes a project delivery manual and detail database, has become a part of daily practice. Computer modeling augments traditional design and presentation methods for study and visualization, as it permits iterative plastic study of forms as well as experimentation with new presentation techniques.

Hardware:

Platforms: a variety of Pentium processor-based PC's. Input Devices: Digital camera, 35mm slide scanner, Flatbed opaque scanner. Output Devices: B&W large format plotters, B&W laser printers, Color large format plotters, color ink-jet printers, Color dye sublimation printer. Storage: Zip drive, CD-ROM reader and writer.

Software:

Within a Microsoft Windows NT operating system, AutoCAD and MicroStation are utilized for drafting and preliminary 3-d studies. 3D Studio Max, Form•Z, Renderzone, Adobe Photoshop and Illustrator, Picture Publisher, and Animator PRO are then utilized to realistically render materials, colors, light and shade.

172

Suburban Mixed-Use Office and Manufacturing Facility. Elgin, Illinois

Suburban Mixed-Use Office, Illinois

▌ Design Concept:

This headquarters complex located on a 130-acre site in Illinois houses light assembly manufacturing, general office, and laboratory space. A glazed pedestrian street organizes the building into clear zones of use, and, by its transparency, blurs the separation of functions. A conference center is experienced as a glass vitrine on the exterior, reflected against the ponds adjacent to the visitor entry. The clean, linear skin of the building's exterior contrasts elegantly with the natural prairie landscape.

▌ Drawing Process/Digital Technique:

The project drawings were produced in AutoCAD and the image was modeled and rendered in 3D Studio Max.

▌ Credits:

Design Team: David Hansen, Randy Guillot, Michael McGeady, Larry Kettelson, Jeff Olson, Diane Zabich.
Rendering: David Dunn

Lynn Classical High School, Massachusetts

▌ Design Concept:

Located in a culturally diverse and dense urban neighborhood, this new school turns inward onto a central commons off which all major spaces are organized and accessed. A light monitor of monumental proportions illuminates the commons with natural light and establishes the building's formal vocabulary.

▌ Drawing Process/Digital Technique:

Partial transparency was employed to view the entirety of the space, as it was conceived. Drawings generated in AutoCAD were imported to 3D Studio, with some added effects generated in Picture Publisher and Animator PRO.

▌ Credits:

Design Team: Ray Bordwell, Mark Chen, Deepika Shrestha Ross, Ann Marie Lewis, Sung-Ho Shin, Christopher Borchardt., Norris McLeod, Mike Poynton, Richard Rosa. Architects of Record: Symmes Maini & McKee Associates, Inc. Cambridge, Massachusetts
Rendering: Sung-Ho Shin

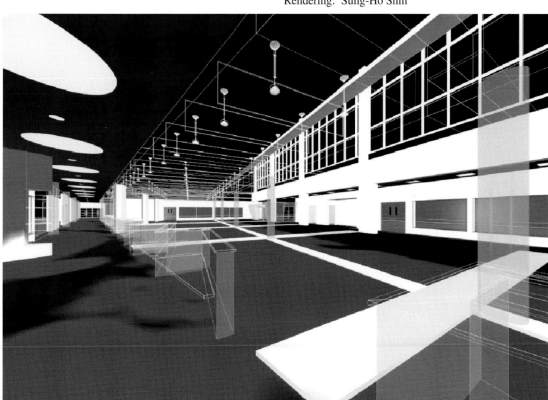

173

Cyber Café, Illinois Institute of Technology, Institute of Design, Chicago, Illinois

Design Concept:

The Cyber Café is an active social environment for the Institute of Design where the incorporation of technology into design stimulates creativity and awareness of perpetual design processes at work in the school. Large write-able screens are capable of displaying video of past student work as well as real-time student design development. Tele/data spheres descend from virtually any location for access to the Internet or the video screens.

Drawing Process/Digital Technique:

Floor plans were drawn and extruded in AutoCAD, then imported into 3D Studio Max where many progressive generations of quick modeling and material studies were developed until one concept was chosen and fine-tuned. Camera angles, lighting effects and scanned images were selected and the final model was rendered and then imported into Photoshop where contrast and color balancing was applied.

Credits:

Design Team:
Carlos Martinez, Jason
Rosenblatt, Kathy Orser.
Rendering: Jason Rosenblatt.

LG Bundang R&D Complex, Bundang, Korea

▌ Design Concept:

Located on a prominent site, the design goals for this research and development project for the LG Group, a progressive international company based in Korea, included the creation of a design that reflects and articulates LG's long term corporate vision of becoming "the best global company."

The facility is comprised of two 25-story towers and a connected 10-story building. Between the two towers a 10-story glass reception atrium invites researchers, guests and visitors into the facility and serves as the formal entry into the complex. Parking and a range of amenities, including a fitness center, cafeteria, and 500-seat auditorium, are located on the 5 levels below grade.

▌ Drawing Process/ Digital Technique:

Computer generated images played an integral part in the many design options studied for this site. A site model was first created to study the context. The images shown here represent initial studies in building form that followed. All digital modeling was executed with AutoCAD r14 and rendered with 3D Studio Max. Photoshop was then used for post rendering effects.

▌ Credits:

Design Team: Ralph Johnson, Bill Doerge, Walter Heffernan, George Beach, Nathalie Belanger, Nicola Casciato, Jin Huh, Charles Killebrew, Monica Oller, David Poorman, David Powell, June Oh, Cengiz Yetken.
Associate Architects: Chang-Jo Architects, Korea
Renderings: David Powell.

Polshek and Partners Architects

E-mail: info@polshek.com
Web Site: www.polshek.com

New York, New York 10014

Oklahoma City Civic Center Music Hall

Profile:

For thirty-five years, Polshek and Partners has created award-winning buildings for cultural, educational, scientific and social service institutions as well as important residential and large-scale industrial buildings and public works. Projects have been published internationally and recognized with numerous awards for design excellence, for their important contributions to the cultural life of the city and for the stabilization of their precincts.

Use of the Digital Media in the Office:

Polshek and Partners Architects has been using digital media since the early 1980's. Digital design has evolved from 3-D wire-frame design models to construction documents and high resolution photorealistic images including animated flythroughs. Currently, the office is using MicroStation SE for its CAD operations, often integrating Adobe Photoshop and QuarkXPress.

Hardware:

Pentium II PC. Output: HP2500

Software:

MicroStation SE was used for plans and sections, MicroStation SE plus Photoshop for 3D images

Drawing Process/Digital Technique:

Microstation color fill over line drawings for plans & sections; MicroStation 3D model renderings with additional manipulation in Photoshop for all 3D images.

Design Concept:

The design for the renovation of the Oklahoma City Civic Center Music Hall converts a 1938 Modeme civic building into a 2500-seat, acoustically ideal "shoe box" theater for the Oklahoma City Philharmonic Orchestra. The project allows the Music Hall to function as a full proscenium theater, incorporating variable acoustics, with fly tower, wings and backstage facilities. This project invents an entirely new architecture that is embedded within the old and interacts with the original in unexpected ways. The volume of the new audience chamber is pulled away from the existing structure and molded into a dynamic form expressive of the performances within. The new theater is connected to the old fabric through a series of circulation elements spanning the interstitial void. Stairs, elevators, ramps and bridges are interspersed through this vast space, creating an exhilarating spatial transformation as one moves from the street through the lobby and atrium to the more mysterious volume of the theater. This journey of discovery into a magnificent and electric space becomes a theatrical event that will be inextricably linked to the cultural life of Oklahoma City. These drawings, which fuse Microstation, and Photoshop appropriately translate the highly technical and complex interstitial relationships between the new and the old architecture.

Credits:

Design Architect: Polshek and Partners Architects LLP
Architect-of-Record: Richard R. Brown Associates

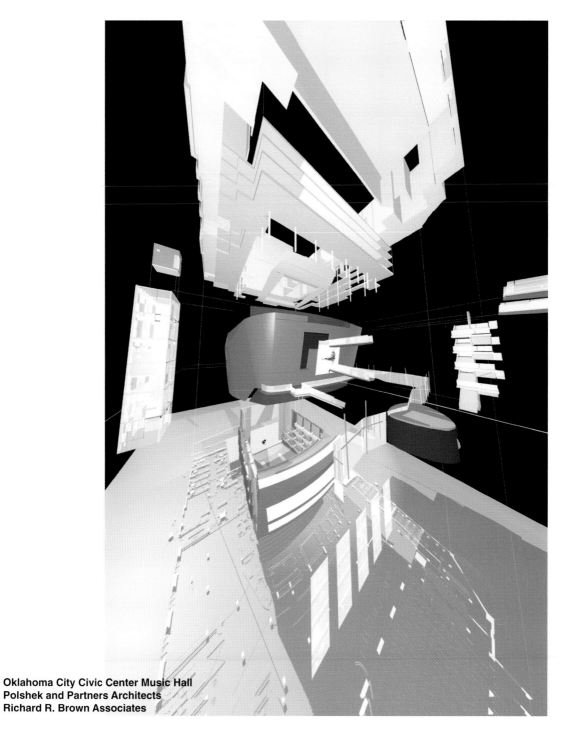

Oklahoma City Civic Center Music Hall
Polshek and Partners Architects
Richard R. Brown Associates

Richard Rauh & Associates, Ltd./Architects

E-mail: rrauh@atlanta.com

Atlanta, Georgia 30318

5th Street Skybridge at Fountain Square, Cincinnati, Ohio
Cinema Renovation, Louisville, Kentucky
Lobby & Entrance, Kenner Toys, Cincinnati, Ohio

Profile:

"We are typically 8-10 people. Buildings designed here have been mostly commercial since the present firm started in 1984. Our core staff learned architecture designing large buildings for real estate developer clients in the 1980's, and has seen a diversity of locations and building types since then. We are licensed to practice in 31 U.S. states. The workplace always has some interns in it, and our environment is set up physically as an open studio in a converted industrial building. Production drafting here transitioned to 100% CAD in the early 90's; all of us are CAD proficient from principal on down."

Richard Rauh's Use of Digital Media:

"Except for in-house design preliminary sketching and concept development, all documentation that we exchange with outsiders is prepared using the usual popular computer applications. This seems to be now standard for anyone who is not working totally alone. It has been a long time since we have seen interns who have hand drawing or lettering skills. We use the internet for sending and receiving data with almost everyone execpt general contractors, though some of them now have digital cameras on the job site. Renderings and presentation work, though prepared on the computer now, has not changed funda-

5th Street Skybridge at Fountain Square, Cincinnati, Ohio

mentally from its age-old function as communication and entertainment for owners, and as stage props that they use to get financing or zoning approvals. Inexplicably though, more students than ever now seem to think that they can make a living doing renderings; this is no more true now than it ever was."

Hardware:

"We have a 14 machine Windows 95/98 network with one NT station and two Unix stations. Our PCs are all Pentium clones that we build ourselves. Many are still housed in old 386 cases that we've re-worked many times over. We are awash in old motherboards, video cards, network cards,

etc. that we can't seem to toss. We have a network post-script printer, several small color inkjet printers, several obsolete dot matrix printers that we use as door stops and of course our trusty HP inkjet plotter. Our monitors are all 17"; our video adapters are variously between 6 months and two years old. We have the usual complement of Zip, CDROM, Jaz drives."

Software:

"Our CAD software is AutoCad 14.0; in the distant past we tried ARRIS and Microstation, but settled into AutoCAD because of client requirements. For rendering we use 3D Studio versions 3,4, and Max, and Photoshop

5th Street Skybridge at Fountain Square, Cincinnati, Ohio

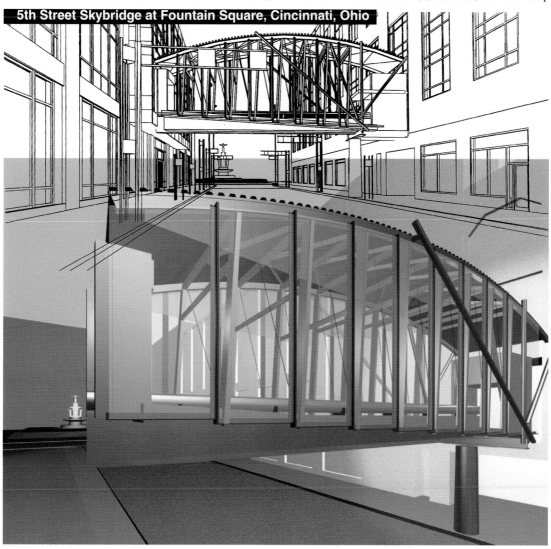

179

release 4.01. We have little use for illustrator software."

■ Drawing Process/Digital Technique:

"Pencil sketching, usually by a principal, precedes creation of initial CAD files, but when dimensioned sketches are necessary CAD drafting is used, sometimes as underlays for pencil sketching. Digital imaging in our office usually happens when a client commissions a picture or rendering or when we simply want to create something for our own purposes. The time/cost investment, it turns out, is almost exactly the same as it is for a hand-built model or a hand-painted rendering. Although owners ask for and expect photorealistic modeling and imaging, we find that digital work that is diagrammatic or conceptual is more satisfying for us. Photorealism seems unnecessary if one is an architect. We find that a digital model that is rendered to look like an architectural model rather than as a full scale

building encourages some owners to think appropriately while the project is in design."

■ Design Concept:

5th Street skybridge at Fountain Square, Cincinnati, Ohio: Unlike other Cincinnati skybridges, this one rests on a single center beam (no view-obstructing side beams) so it can have glass all around. The floor slopes as it crosses the street, enveloping the center beam. The arched roof frames the axis down Fifth Street to the city's famous Tyler Davidson Fountain and resolves the unequal window height conditions at the new Federated Department store (Lazarus) in downtown Cincinnati.

Cinema Renovation, St. Mathews, Louisville, Kentucky: This twenty-year-old, eight screen movie theatre built underneath a tennis club had its HVAC system units outside on a rusting entrance marquee. The new design uses dramatic lighting and an inexpensive corrugated metal and translucent fiberglass shell to wrap the external systems into a geometry that has a scale meant to be arresting from the highway.

Cinema Renovation, Louisville, Kentucky

180

Design Concept:

Lobby & Entrance, Kenner Toys, Cincinnati, Ohio: The lobby/entrance design of the Kenner Toys/Hasbro corporate building on the east side of downtown Cincinnati near the Procter and Gamble world headquarters. Suspended and cantilevered structural steel supports entrance canopy of corrugated steel and thin limestone panels.

Credits:

Richard Rauh & Associates, Ltd. / Architects
Atlanta, Georgia

Lobby & Entrance, Kenner Toys, Cincinnati, Ohio

Resolution: 4 Architecture

Web Site: www.re4a.com

New York, New York 10001

Zao Fong Universe Building, Shanghai, China
Freimark Residence, North Caldwell, New Jersey
McCann Erickson Advertising Agency Screening Room, New York, New York

Profile:

The office of 'Resolution: 4 Architecture' believes that architecture is the realization of a conceptual landscape that has the potential to uncover and describe the incomplete nature of things. Architecture establishes relationships between form, use, materials, and meanings, and ultimately expresses an idea and the uniqueness of each client. It becomes an intentional response that connects/disconnects similar or disparate elements. It goes beyond the capability of words and drawings. With this understanding, the office strives to produce work that is both meaningful and useful, and which also has purpose within the larger context. Founded in 1990, Resolution: 4 Architecture is a young office in New York comprised of partners Joseph Tanney and Robert Luntz, and a small staff of talented and dedicated architects.

Use of Digital Media in the Office:

The use of digital media at Resolution: 4 permeates all stages of a project's life. During the initial schematic design stage, computer-aided 3-D design informs planiometric computer drawings and vice versa, giving a more holistic understanding of how a design is working. As the design progresses, renderings of computer models and prints of planimetric drawings are presented to the client as the design is updated. The construction documents are a completely digitized set of planometric drawings, which are printed out in hard copy form and given to contractors and other groups at the time they are needed for review, permit, or construction.

Hardware:

'Resolution: 4 Architecture' is currently using the MacOS platform with several Macintosh PowerPC's and G3's. Output devices range from Epson color printers to Hewlett Packard Design Jet.

Software:

The main software packages used at Resolution:4 are MiniCAD 7.1 for planometrics, Form•Z 2.9 for computer modeling, Photoshop 4.0 for site photos and rendering touch-ups, and QuarkXPress 4.0 for presentation layouts.

Drawing Process/Digital Technique:

Initially, projects are produced in MiniCAD based on free-hand sketches. Generally, digitally created rendered images, which are presented to clients, start in Form•Z as wire-frame constructions that are subsequently rendered by using the software's own rendering program: RenderZone. The rendered models are saved as images as PICT format in Form•Z to be opened in Photoshop, where adjustments are made. Saved in TIFF format in Photoshop, the images can be placed in QuarkXPress documents were further augmentation (usually text) occurs. Final documents are either printed for use in house for design purposes or client meetings, saved on disks for output elsewhere perhaps to be used by a third party, or placed directly on Resolution: 4's web page, where they remain in digital form and are often incorporated as a QuickTime VR (see Freimark series print).

182

Zao Fong Universe Building, Shanghai, China

Zao Fong Universe Building , Shanghai, China

Concept:

The gateway to this "Universe" is a stainless steel canopy, which contains lighted planes, to make a transition from the outside into the Zao Fong Universe. The wedge-shaped canopy provides light and floats above the sidewalk, while sheltering visitors, to imply flying, or floating, into the building.

Credits:

Project Team: Joseph Tanney, Robert Luntz, Gary Shoemaker, Eric Lifton.
Digital Rendering: Eric Lifton

McCann Erickson Advertising Agency Screening Room, New York, New York

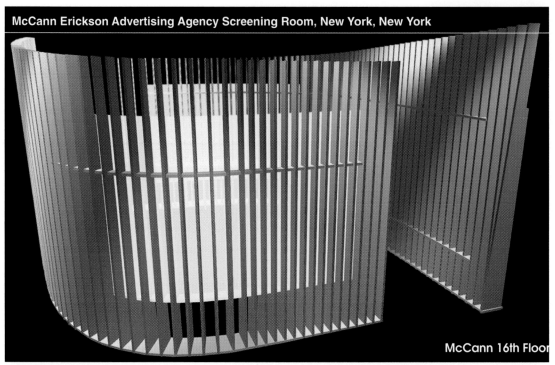

McCann 16th Floor

Concept: As part of a larger context, a video screening room acts as an event moment, by which two intersecting planes begin to form a spatial "cup" both horizontally and vertically.

McCann Erickson Advertising Agency Conference Room, New York, New York

McCann 20th Floor

Concept: This project is about defining a horizontal space by using a system of object repetition and reflection. It is a system by which an object can create a void through a series of moves.

Credits:
Project Team: Joseph Tanney, Robert Luntz, Clayton Collier, Mario Gentile, Mike Sweebe, Michael Syracuse.
Digital Rendering: Brian Bowman, Mike Sweebe

Freimark Residence, North Caldwell, New Jersey

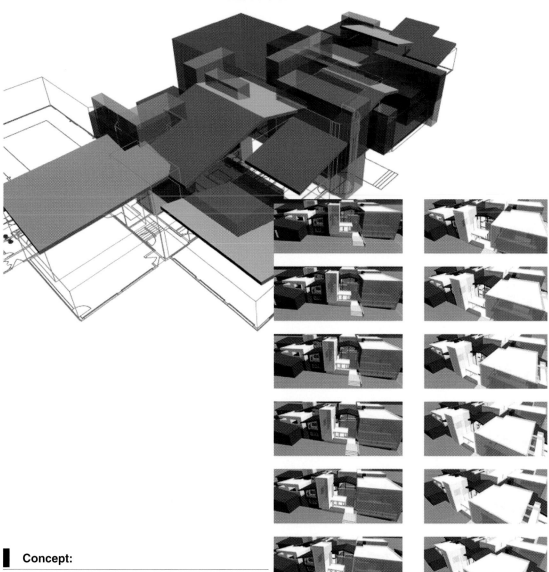

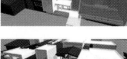

Concept:

This project consists of an existing condition of undulating roof planes that are to receive new functions as volumes inserted within a bobbing system and grouped around a central vertical core of space.

Credits:

Project Team: Joseph Tanney, Robert Luntz, Erin Vali, Roy Leone, Jason Buchheit, Brock Danner.
Digital Rendering: Brian Bowman

Rogers Marvel Architects

Web Site: Pending
E-mail: rmarch@aol.com
New York, New York 10013

Addition to the South Fork Natural History Society Museum, Bridgehampton, NY
Higgins Hall, Pratt Institute, Brooklyn, New york

Profile:

Rogers Marvel Architects was formed by Robert Rogers and Jonathan Marvel in 1992. Both had experience in larger, high profile offices working on museums and institutional projects; the office was formed from a desire to seek their own direction. Recent projects include additions to the Studio Museum in Harlem, El Museo del Barrio, the South Fork Natural History Society Museum, and the Architecture School at Pratt Institute.

Use of Digital Media at Rogers Marvel:

"Since much of our work includes major renovations, we constantly inhabit the ends of the spectrum of extreme abstraction and realistic color rendering. We explore the broad concept and test refined insertions."

Hardware and Software:

Hardware: P.C.-compatible CPUs, scanner with transparency adapter, high-end photo-quality inkjet printer, laser printer.

Software: Form•Z with RenderZone, Photoshop, Quark XPress.

Drawing Process / IDigital Technique:

Initial schematic sketches are done combining computer drawings and physical models. The models are photographed and used in digital collage to study the project's relationship to the existing building and site. The design is then refined through computer perspectives, orthogonal projections, and planning diagrams. The final design is rendered in both physical model and computer imaging using rendering packages.

186

Addition to the South Fork Natural History Society Museum, Bridgehampton, New York

The South Fork Natural History Museum Bridgehampton, New York

▌ Concept:

The South Fork Natural History Museum will occupy the former Bridgehampton Winery. The two existing structures for museum exhibitions and support services will be powered by photovoltaic panels. An experimental observation tower and reception hall will be built between two original elements of the winery, and will act as a year round connector. It will serve as a 'front door' to indoor displays and for the nature and preserve wildlife beyond.

▌ Credits:

Project Design Team: Jonathan Marvel, Robert Rogers, Camilo Cerro, Vincent Lee.

Pratt Institute School of Architecture: Higgins Hall Brooklyn, New York

▌ Concept:

Pratt Institute selected Rogers Marvel Architects to reconstruct the School of Architecture at Higgins Hall after a devastating fire in July 1996. The reconstruction will be completed in three phases: the stabilization of the damaged North Wing envelope; a complete interior renovation to the North Wing; and an entirely new Central Wing to be designed with Steven Holl Architects. New work in the North Wing will echo the interior spatial openings in the existing South Wing, yet extend the spatial vocabulary to new, selectively exposed, building systems. This renovation anticipates the insertion of the glass Central Wing, which will connect the two wings spatially and conceptually.

▌ Credits:

Project Design Team: Jonathan Marvel, Robert Rogers, Marcel Granier, James Hartford, Guido Hartaray, Carol Patterson, Bodil Pedersen.

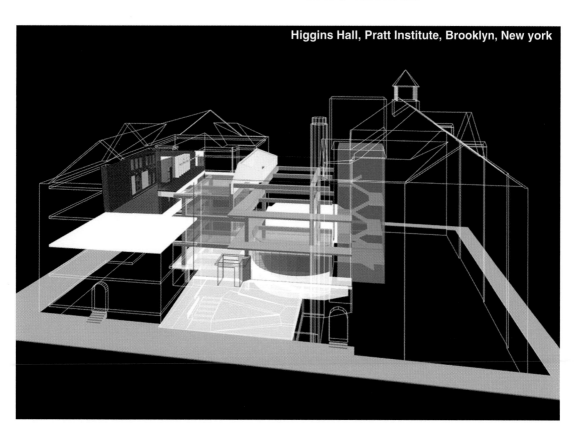

Higgins Hall, Pratt Institute, Brooklyn, New york

SCHWARTZ Architects

e-mail: ASAPNYC@aol.com

New York, New York 10014

East End Rep Co., Amagansett, Long Island, New York
Staten Island Ferry Terminal, New York, New York

▍Profile:

Frederic Schwartz was a recipient of the prestigious Rome Prize in Architecture and a National Endowment for the Arts Design Fellowship. He graduated Phi Beta Kappa from the University of California at Berkeley in 1973 and received a Master of Architecture from Harvard University in 1978. Mr. Schwartz has taught architectural design at Princeton University, Columbia University, Harvard University, Yale University, and the Universities of Miami, North Carolina, Pennsylvania, and Milan. He has lectured on his work throughout America and Europe. Mr. Schwartz has won a number of major design competitions, including the new Staten Island Ferry Terminal and Peter Minuit Park at the tip of Manhattan, the new Southwest Regional Capitol of France in Toulouse (joint venture w/ Ventury, Scott Brown & Associates nearing completion) and the new East End Repertory Theater in Amagansett. He has designed a number of award winning houses and his work has been shown in various national and interna-

tional exhibitions. Schwartz is also the author of three books: *Mother's House,* by Rizzoli (English, Japanese, German); *Alan Buchsbaum: the Mechanics of Taste,* by Monacelli Press; and *Venturi, Scott Brown Associates,* by Zanichelli (Italian, English, Spanish, German).

▍Use of Digital Media in the Office:

Schwartz Architects uses computers and digital media as a way of conveying ideas. Every desk is a computerized workstation. However, the office is not a paperless environment. In-house large format presentation boards are quickly produced with color digital imaging not previously affordable. The client has a tangible product and is not faced with a virtual computer screen image. The office also has invested in scanning technology to more easily deal with both pre-existing graphic and text information. The images presented of the Staten Island Ferry Terminal and East End Rep Co. exemplify this methodology.

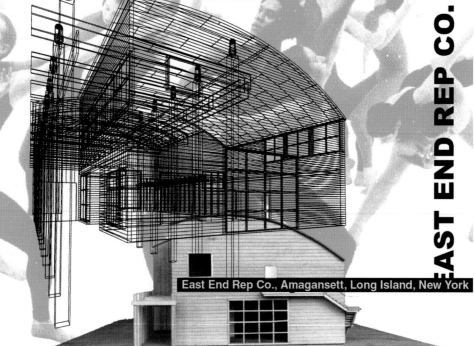

East End Rep Co., Amagansett, Long Island, New York

188

Hardware:

The Staten Island Ferry Terminal graphics were compiled on a variety of Dell Pentium II computers. The whole system is networked on an Ethernet Windows NT platform utilizing a Dell network server. An Agfa flatbed scanner capable of scanning both transparent and opaque material is a fundamental part of the system. Finally for output, the office uses an Epson large format color Ink-Jet printer as well as a high output Hewlett-Packard Laser Jet printer.

Software:

AutoCAD Release 14, 3D Studio Max, scanning software, and Adobe Photoshop 4.0.

Drawing Process/Digital Technique:

All of the images presented were compiled in the following manner. AutoCAD Release 14 was used to model the actual building. 3D Studio Max was then used to render the AutoCAD model. Rendered images were then collaged with a variety of scanned images (some from actual site photographs and some from hand drawings) using Adobe Photoshop 4.0. Images such as view of the Staten Island Ferry Terminal are the combination of a Digital model and actual site photographs. However the nighttime image was originally a hand drawn rending for a previous scheme. Instead of losing the rendering the image was scanned in and the old hand drawn design was replaced by a new computer model.

Staten Island Ferry Terminal, New York, New York

Credits:

Architect-in-Charge: Frederic Schwartz.
Project Director: Ronald Evitts.
Associate-in-charge: Paul Cali.
Design Team: John Adams, Inness Asaman, Felicity Beck, Chris Broshears, Linna Choi, Dae-ik Kim, Leslie Kim, Kimberlae Saul and David Tepper.

189

TRO/The Ritchie Organization
Web Site: http://www.troarch.com

Newton, Massachusetts 02158

Philippines Medical center, Manila Philippines

Profile:

TRO/The Ritchie Organization is an award-winning, 180-person architectural/engineering firm headquartered in Newton, Massachusetts. With services ranging, from real estate asset management to master planning, space programming, architectural, interior design and engineering. TRO's volume of work has encompassed over 400 clients throughout the world with construction projects totaling more than $ 3.5 billion. Together with its award-winning healthcare design, which has been a specialty for more than 45 years, TRO also provides innovative design solutions to a growing list of corporate and educational clients.

Use of Digital Media:

The use of computers in TRO goes beyond drafting to the broader realm of design and information technology. 3D visualization has become an important tool to better understand design and make more informed decisions. Depending, on a project's and client's need, the use of digital media involves creating series of 3D rendered images, animations, and more recently, teaming up with a multimedia consultant to produce an interactive CD-ROM.

Hardware:

Systems consist of PC based Pentium II systems with 128 MB of RAM and 3D graphic accelerator cards. For pre-

sentation purposes TRO is using laptop computers with video projectors.

Software:

TRO uses a Windows NT platform with the following software: AutoCAD, Form•Z, 3D Studio Max; Photoshop, QuarkXPress, Adobe Premiere, PowerPoint, and Director. In addition, the firm is using variety of 3D model, image and sound libraries for use with digital images/animations.

Drawing Process/Image Technique:

3D modeling and imagery are an integral part of the design process. In the early design stages, 3D computer diagrams are a crucial tool in perspective massing studies as well as understanding the inner forces and circulation adjacencies within. While the project progresses, the 3D diagram evolves into a building with a defined wall fenestration and ultimately includes materials and textures.

Design Concept:

The design team responded to the challenge by creating a medical "city" that accommodates the full spectrum of both medical and diagnostic services under one roof. The building has been carefully sited to optimize ease of access, parking and entry. The design utilizes a universal grid and modular planning, consolidates core services and optimizes building support systems and floor plates to achieve a higher net-to-gross ratio, thereby reducing the overall building area and volume. This promotes maximum flexibility and results in lowered maintenance and operational costs.

Credits:

Architect: TRO/The Ritchie Organization
Principal-in-Charge: Brendan Morrisroe
Design Principal: Carlos Melendez, AIA
Project Designer: Andrzej Zarzycki
Project Planner: Tom Lam, AIA
Project Coordinator: Segundo Gilladoga
Computer Graphics: Andrzej Zarzycki
TRO Contact: Brendan Morrisroe

Philippines Medical Center Worldwide Capital/Phil-Asia Group, Manila, Philippines

Tsao & McKown Architects

E-Mail: tsao@tsao-mckown.com

New York, Singapore

Hugo Boss Sport

Profile:

Tsao & McKown is a New York based firm with an office in Singapore. The firm has earned an international reputation for its ability to transform complex building projects, such as the $1.6 billion Suntec City in Singapore, into architecture memorable for its humanity, attention to detail, and embrace of diversity. The work also includes many smaller projects considered significant, among them interior design for Ian Schrager's Morgans Hotel in New York; McCord museum interiors in Montreal; high-fashion department stores and other retail projects including the Geoffrey Beene boutique in New York; in addition to: apartment and townhouse interiors; various restaurants; and objects ranging from much-copied sinks and bathtubs to dinnerware, candlesticks, and picture frames sold at the Museum of Modern Art. Set designs for dance, museum exhibitions, fashion presentations, and film design continue to be critical aspects of the firm's practice.

The practice of Tsao & McKown is a constant process of inquiry, affirmation, and critical speculation. In this sense Tsao & McKown is part of a new school that does not believe in stylistic imprints or strive to make consumers of clients. The firm seeks instead a simplicity that is not reductive and a clarity that is not solely a matter of form. The means is a process of distillation rather than Cartesian models. What appears "stylish" about the work evolves from a very studied, earnest, and arduous process of research and gathering facts. What is unique derives from culture.

Use of Digital Media:

The digital media is used for the purpose of efficient visual communication and the exploring "possibilities" and approximating their reality.

Hardware and Software:

Hardware: Macintoshs operating systems and Windows NT stations.

Software: Form•Z for modeling, Illustrator and Photoshop for graphics, and AutoCAD for working drawings.

Drawing Process/Image Technique:

The process includes: Idea/Sketches/Computer model/ Working model/1:1 model - mockup (when it is possible)/ Revisions/Computer model.

Computer Model is a quick illustration of an idea. It is used in combination with other methods, like image collages (visual abstraction of the idea) and material collages (tactile abstraction of the idea).

Design Concept:

Hugo Boss Sport: The identity of the soon to be launched Hugo Boss Sport's is differentiated by the fact that it draws on European urbanity and country life, and Europe's more sophisticated sports traditions, such as skiing and sailing. The resulting Hugo Boss Sport design concept is comprised of an eclectic mix of elements, utilizing varied colors and forms, but unified by their common derivation from a good understanding of the gestalt of European leisure.

So, somewhat in the spirit of an old rural retreat that has been lovingly transformed over time and updated with the latest technologies; the overall effect of Hugo Boss Sport, with its rustic wooden floors and stationer's inspired simple metal shelving will strike sympathetic chords of shared memories.

For example, the round red leather sofa was morphed from a racing car seat. The result is something new and original, a step into the future perhaps; but the reference is at least felt, if not recognized with a smile. Similarly, there is a delightful sense of recall, plus pleasure in recognizing something new, when an old-fashioned leather punching bag is here rendered in new materials and then transformed to become the dressing room seat.

Credits:

Client: Hugo Boss AG
Architect: Tsao & McKown Architects
Design team: Calvin Tsao, Adam Rolston, Kyo Chin, Jill Edelman, Thomas Bargetz, Erika Ratvay

Copyright by Hugo Boss AG, 1998

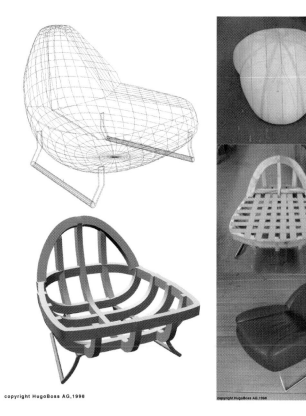

copyright HugoBoss AG,1998

copyright HugoBoss AG,1998

Bernard Tschumi Architects

Web Site: www.tschumi.com

New York, Paris

Lerner Student Center, Columbia University, New York, New York
K•polis Department Store, Zürich, Switzerland, 1995 International Competition
Le Fresnoy National Studio for Contemporary Arts, Tourcoing, France

Profile:

Bernard Tschumi's projects have been widely published and exhibited internationally and are the subject of frequent discussion, to which he himself has contributed with four books, including *The Manhattan Transcripts* (1981; re-printed in 1994, Rizzoli), *Architecture and Disjunction* (1994, The MIT Press), and *Event-Cities* (1994, The MIT Press), the latter published on the occasion of the exhibition *Bernard Tschumi: Architecture and Event* at The Museum of Modern Art in New York.

Major built projects include the Parc de la Villette, Paris (125-acre), Le Fresnoy Art and Film Center in Tourcoing, Lerner Student Center in New York, the School of Architecture in Marne-la-Vallée (under construction).

Bernard Tschumi is also dean of New York's Columbia University Graduate School of Architecture, Planning and Preservation.

Use of Digital Media:

The office uses digital media as an integral part of the design process, from initial conceptual and formal studies, through architectural elaboration and structural studies, to drawing production and final renderings. The office has also increasingly used the internet as a source for information and inspiration as well as an outlet for presenting ideas.

Hardware:

The office uses a network of primarily Macintosh computers, a color large-format plotter, high-resolution medium-format inkjet printer, laser printer, as well as a scanner.

Software:

The office uses Minicad for two-dimensional drafting, Form•Z for modeling and design studies, and ElectricImage for presentation rendering and animation. QuarkXPress, and Photoshop are used for graphic design and image refinement. Communicator and Fetch are used to connect to the internet and to send files between offices.

Lerner Student Center, Columbia University

Drawing Process / Image Technique:

Top Image: This image was created at a point where we were using the software to study how the structure of the glass ramps (on the right) affected the spatial sense of the "hub", and the transmission of light and views from the outside. It was rendered in ElectricImage.

Bottom Image: This image of the "hub" was based on a highly detailed Form•Z model of the student center. The model lighting was carefully set up to match actual fixture locations and characteristics, and give a realistic and dramatic night view. It was rendered in ElectricImage.

Concept:

The new Student Center at Columbia University acts as a forum, a dynamic place of exchange. Its multiple activities, from its 1500-seat combined auditorium and cinema to its meeting rooms, dining halls, game rooms, student clubs and, bookstore, are to be perceived from the series of oblique lounges that link the multiplicity of disparate functions into a new University "event." By analogy, the student center could be described as a dynamic hub that acts as a major social space.

Acting as the building's core, the Hub is made possible by the unusual condition of much of the Columbia campus at this location, where the campus side is half a story higher than the neighborhood (Broadway) side.

Credits:

Lerner Student Center, Columbia University, New York, New York.
Architect: Bernard Tschumi Architects/ Gruzen Samton Associated Architects.

Design Team (BTA): Bernard Tschumi, Tom Kowalski, Mark Haukos, Ruth Berktold, Megan Miller, Kim Starr, Richard Veith, Galia Solomonoff, Yannis Aesopos, Anthony Manzo, Peter Cornell, Jordan Parnass, Frederick Norman.

LERNER STUDENT CENTER, COLUMBIA UNIVERSITY

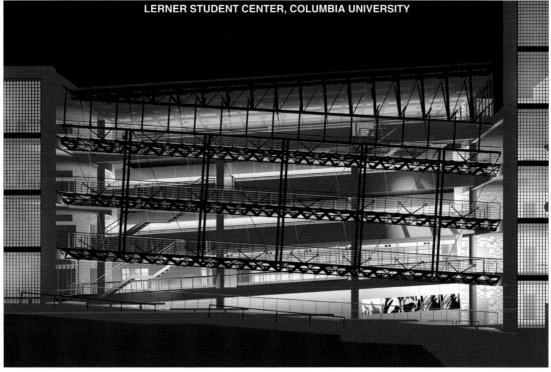

LERNER STUDENT CENTER, COLUMBIA UNIVERSITY

K•polis Department Store, Zürich, Switzerland 1995 International Competition

▌ Concept:

Architecture of Display - Display of Architecture

Department stores and museums share one thing in common: the need for seduction through a language of display. Each exposed product becomes an object of desire. Walking is the preferred means to apprehend these objects of desire. A slow dance begins between two bodies: the dynamic body of the viewing visitor/consumer and the static body of the object of consumption.

In the project for the new K•polis, the architects have tried to express this dance. A ramp ascends in a random manner and intersects all parts of the building. Like a long vector of movement, the ramp activates the buildings, defines intensity and areas of use. It is the main street of the Polis, it is open at late hours, and it is the route of the New. All the new products are displayed along the ramp.

▌ Credits:

Architect: Bernard Tschumi Architects
Design Team: Bernard Tschumi, Gregory Merryweather, Niels Roefs, Ruth Berktold, Tom Kowalski, Mark Haukos, Kevin Collins

Le Fresnoy National Studio for Contemporary Arts, Tourcoing, France

▌ Concept:

Strategy of the In-Between

A school, a film studio, a mediathèque, spectacle and exhibition halls, two cinemas, laboratories for research and production (sound, electronic image, film and video), administrative offices, housing and a bar / restaurant: this is the multiple program of the new center.

If the new roof over old and new parts acts as the project's common denominator (a large screen-umbrella), the architects also sought to accelerate the probability of chance events in the in-between by combining diverse elements (the meeting of umbrella and sewing machine on the dissecting table), juxtaposing great roof, school / research laboratory and the old Fresnoy, place of spectacle.

Award: 1996 Grand Prix National d'Architecture (French Ministry of Culture)

▌ Credits:

Project: Le Fresnoy National Studio for Contemporary Arts, Tourcoing, France

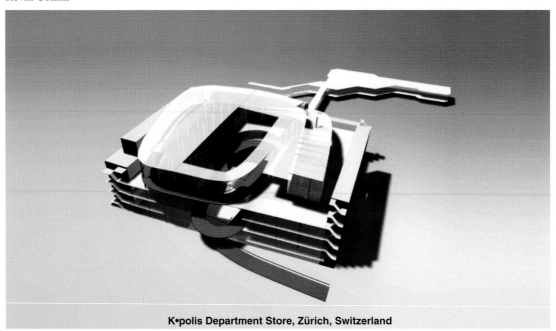

K•polis Department Store, Zürich, Switzerland

Architect: Bernard Tschumi Architects

Design Team: Bernard Tschumi, Tom Kowalski, Jean-François Erhel, Véronique Descharrières, François Gillet, Mark Haukos, Yannis Aesopos, Henning Ehrhart.

Structural Engineering: Tetraserf
Mechanical Engineering: Choulet
Site Coordinator: S.C.O.
Quantity Surveyor: Fouché
Interior Designer: Bernard Tschumi Architects
Main Contractor: SOGEA
Photographers: Peter Mauss/ESTO, Robert Cesar, Bernard Tschumi Architects

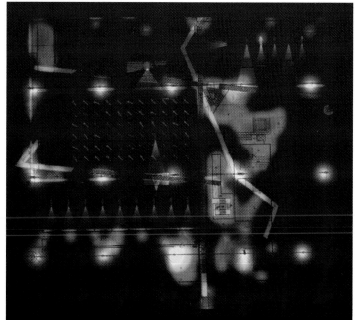

Le Fresnoy National Studio for ContemporaryArts, Tourcoing, France

197

van Dijk Pace Westlake Architects Web Site: www.vpwa.com

Cleveland, Ohio 44115 • Phoenix, Arizona 85012

Travel Center of America Prototype, current construction in 12 states

Profile:

Services: Comprehensive design and management services including Architecture, Interior Architecture and Design, Master Planning, Programming, Feasibility Studies, Construction Management and Engineering.

Ownership: A Limited Liability Company (LLC) with five members: Peter van Dijk, FAIA, Richard Y. Pace, AIA, Paul Westlake Jr., FAIA, Ronald Reed, AIA, Vince Leskosky, AIA

Established: In continuous practice since 1905

Number of Employees: Approximately 100 technical and support staff

Annual Volume: Approximately $500,000,000 in construction value in design

Recognitions: More than 100 design awards, including the AIA Ohio Gold Medal

Specialties: Academic Facilities, Adaptive Reuse, Historic Preservation, Corporate Facilities, Cultural Facilities, Environments for Older Adults, Healthcare Facilities, Urban Design and Planning , Design / Build.

Use of the Digital Media in the Office:

van Dijk Pace Westlake Architects have been using computers in design processes since 1986. Initially, CAD drawings were introduced to enhance design communications, specifically in streamlining the production of working drawings. Within a short time van Dijk Pace Westlake had defined its commitment to the use of technological resources and began to leverage those resources to further client communications and promote business development.

In particular, the use of digital imaging resources are a constant in the firm's design processes. Three-dimensional modeling and rendering are offered as a service to clients

at the initial concept stages of design. It allows clients to make informed decisions about design concepts and involves them in the design process. This service allows clients to communicate effectively with investors and other decision making executives at critical developmental stages.

In addition to three-dimensional modeling and rendering, van Dijk Pace Westlake Architects produces digital graphics, including two-dimensional graphics studies; enhanced digital imaging, especially design studies and presentations with photographs; digital slide show presentations in marketing and as a client service; and computer animations.

Hardware:

Each workstation is equipped with appropriate PC based hardware including a minimum of 32 MB RAM, a CD-ROM, a Zip Drive, and a 20 inch color monitor. Several high-performance workstations are continually upgraded and are accessible for larger, more intricate modeling and imaging projects. The Cleveland and Phoenix offices have equal hardware capabilities and are linked by a wide-area network allowing for seamless collaboration on projects from geographically diverse locations.Each of the offices also has on its local network a high-resolution scanner, 11x17 color inkjet printer, and large format HP color printers.

Software:

Each staff workstation has access to a variety of digital imaging software including AutoCAD R14, AccuRender, Form•Z, 3D Studio, Adobe Photoshop, Adobe PageMaker, Microsoft Office products, and Internet access.

Drawing Process/Digital Technique:

Each 3-dimensional model and computer generated rendering is preceded by traditional design processes. Hand sketches drawn on tracing paper are augmented with

198

graphic images xeroxed onto transparent adhesive are scanned into Photoshop and color and additional graphics are added to create 2-dimensional collages. Mass models are constructed both in wood or cardboard as well as in the 3-dimensional computer environment. These models are studied and graphic pieces from the original collage are applied to the massing model. Final design decisions are made and the 3D model is further developed to its final form. The renderings are purposely not intended to be photo-realistic. The firm finds that when the computer generated drawings are more abstract and broad-brush than real and representative, they are received more enthusiastically by the client, leading to discussions of design concepts rather than the minutia of the detail in the rendering.

Design Concept:

Designed as a gesture towards America's motorized culture and roadside landscape, the 30,000 square foot travel center prototype balances the needs of both professional drivers and motorists. The design breaks down tariffs and barriers between the professional drivers and the motorists, or 'four-wheelers.' Early concepts included the submersion of a chromed eighteen-wheel truck cab in the facade of the fast food wing. This embedded truck was to function as a 'playland' for motorists' children. The pick-up window continues this theme as burgers are loaded out of the 'back' of the truck trailer. The blue, white, and red striped awning which dominates the restaurant wing is a parody of the well-recognized icon for roadside franchise dining. The combination of the sweeping vault and pylon serve to both identify and unify TravelCenters of America's network of new and existing facilities.

Credits:

van Dijk Pace Westlake Architects, Cleveland.
Karen Skunta & Company

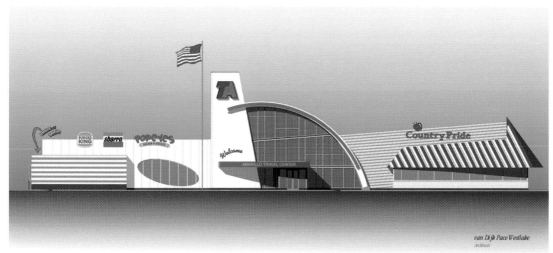

van Dijk Pace Westlake
Architects

199

Venturi, Scott Brown and Associates

Web Site: www.vsba.com
E-mail: info@vsba.com

Philadelphia, Pennsylvania 19127

Whitehall Ferry Terminal, New york, New York

Profile:

In the past 34 years of practice, Venturi, Scott Brown and Associates has earned an international reputation as one of the world's leading architectural design and planning firms. Through influential work in these disciplines as well as in decorative arts and theoretical writing, the firm-under the leadership of Robert Venturi and Denise Scott Brown-has helped transform contemporary architecture and is regarded as a driving force in the shaping of late twentieth-century design.

VSBA is a 58-person office but a "one-team firm" where the principals are involved in each major project from beginning to end. They are supported by a staff of 21 registered architects, some of whom have been with the firm almost 30 years. VSBA's current projects include a student center at Princeton University; a second laboratory building at UCLA, two library projects at Dartmouth College; and a master plan and student-center complex at the University of Pennsylvania and campus master planning for the University of Michigan. Internationally, VSBA is currently working on a regional administrative and legislative center in Toulouse, France.

Use of the Digital Media in the Office:

Because the firm generates its designs from the individual imperatives and opportunities of each project, each of the completed works has its own unique identity derived from a careful consideration of the philosophy of its client, the traditions of the institution, the requirements of the program and the characteristics of the site. Digital media in the office generally consist of 2-D renderings produced on large format plotters for presentation to individual clients. The office also produces QuickTime videos and 3-D renderings for special purposes.

Hardware:

Workstations are equipped with appropriate PC based hardware including Dual PentiumII processors with 256MB RAM, desktop scanners, laser printers, and plotters.

Software:

Staff workstations have access to a variety of digital imaging software including AutoCAD, Adobe Photoshop, Adobe Illustrator, Microsoft Office, and appropriate Internet access software. Software used for illustrated images consists of Adobe Photoshop and Illustrator.

Drawing Process/Digital Technique:

Image techniques includes Adobe Photoshop montage of model photo with site photo.

Design Concept:

In an era when civic space has been supplanted by shopping centers, the new Whitehall Ferry Terminal is an unparalleled opportunity to create a civic setting that celebrates New York City and enhances the daily routine of 70,000 commuters.

This winning competition entry acknowledges the terminal as the first and last building on Manhattan Island and accommodates at the same time the diversity of its context-social, cultural and architectural. A giant clock was chosen as a classic symbol of civic architecture on the harbor facade, its generous size in scale with the towering skyline behind it. The section of the building has an upsweep toward the north to frame the immediate view of Lower Manhattan from the inside, and a parapeted, flag-shaped electronic billboard on the water-facing south facade. The wavy curves of the profile of this facade prevent it from looking like a billboard and work also to contrast it with the rectangle dominated composition of its skyline "backdrop." Its electronic LED images change and move, and can include ornament, pattern, information and color, though the predominant image is of a waving fragment of a flag, perceived from afar across a bay.

Credits:

Venturi, Scott Brown and Associates, Inc.
and Anderson/Schwartz Architects; TAMS Consultants, Inc.

200

VISTAARA Architects

E-mail: delvista@bdmail.net

Dhaka, Bangladesh

Bashundhara City, Dhaka, Bangladesh

Profile:

Vistaara is a conglomeration of architects and engineers with varied experiences. It believes that the spirit of exclusiveness lie in an unconventional understanding of aesthetics and functionality which emanates from one's intuitive fitness. The international atmosphere, be it technology or culture, considerably influence architecture to attain a more internationalized direction, but at the same time, Vistaara exerts experimentation with construction and materials, architectural elements of formal expression like planes, geometry, mass, shape and volume more responsive to unique contexts. With this in mind, Vistaara has been offering its distinguished and definitive statement in the architectural realm of Bangladesh since 1988. Besides the ultimate output of architectural pieces, Vistaara has established itself as the most advanced architectural enterprise in Bangladesh having decided authority in computer modeling, drawing and simulation. The digital creations have compelled Vistaara not only to be the technically sound organisation but to a prompt and enduring service provider in this country.

Vistaara's Use Digital Media:

Vistaara is totally computerized. After being commissioned a project, the obvious initial strokes on the concept are transformed into 3D modelling to produce the first tangible output. Vistaara's first judgement of the project is conveyed to the client in a simple presentation in its office with the help of those rendered 3D models with the intention to develop an understanding of the visual and spatial possibilities of the project. After the formal aspects of the project are finalized in such an appraisement, the functional possibilities of the project are translated into computer drawings showing plans and layouts and ultimately the refined version of 3D model is rendered and touched with graphics software. The updated design comprising rendered images and drawings is followed by the starting of the process of preparing construction documents in computer aided design software. The hardcopies of the images and drawings are printed out in plotter.

Hardware:

Vistaara has dedicated a single IBM PC to each user ranging from the designers to the CAD operators and each PC is brought under the local area network to facilitate the users sharing of files and efficient use of the machines. Output devices range from Canon and Epson color printers to Hewlett Packard's LaserJet and Design Jet. Scanning device is Hewlett Packard's HP ScanJet. Canon copier is used for reproductive purpose.

Software:

AutoCAD R14 is used for 2D drawings and 3D-mesh constructions, 3D MAX 2 to rendering the mesh for virtual imaging and also for certain 3D-mesh constructions. Adobe Photoshop 5.0 is used for enhancing the virtual effects of the rendered images and for photomontage and Corel Draw 8.0 for presentation.

Drawing Process/Digital Technique:

Upon the conceptual design the first 2D drawing is produced for the base plan in AutoCAD R14 accommodating the functional possibilities of the project. The basic 3D-wire-mesh is then generated on the basis of the base plan. The volumetric aspect of the architecture is then understood from different angle and subsequently adjusted for achieving best result. In the process of developing the 3D Model, it is exported in DXF format to 3DS Max for several times and rendered with material and shadow maps to understand the virtual effect of the project. The virtual image is studied thoroughly and rectified in AutoCAD. After the fine-tuning, the final 3D mesh is then again exported in DXF format for final rendering in 3DS Max, where materials and background are assigned as per design. The rendered image is then saved in .TIF format and retouched in Adobe Photoshop. To present to the client the image is layered with human figures, trees, cars etc. The output is then preserved both for the design documentation phase and the client.

▌ Design Concept:

Bashundhara City: The largest single structure of Bangladesh accommodates 3500 shops, amusement and health facilities and commercial tower. The basic concept of the design is derived from the Hindu Myth of nine squares, where the central square acts as the womb and others are survived upon it. Cruciform spine leading to the central court produces a converging psychodrama that in turn makes the building into a meeting place. The street facades are sculpted out at human scale so that it produces a more democratic piece of architecture.

▌ Credits:

Project Team: Mustapha Khalid, M. Foyezullah and Shahzia Islam.
Digital Rendering: Mustapha Khalid, M. Foyezullah

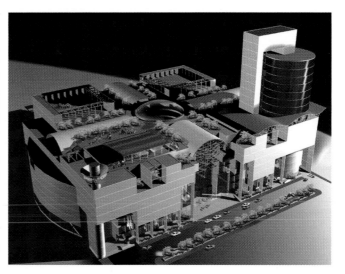

203

Voorsanger & Associates Architects

E-mail: Voorarch@aol.com
Web Site: www.BVArchitect.com

New York, New York 10018

Asia Society, New York, New York

Profile:

Bartholomew Voorsanger graduated with honors from Princeton University in 1960, received a University fellowship to study in France at the Ecole des Beaux-Arts de Fontainebleau in 1961, and earned a Masters of Architecture from Harvard University Graduate School of Design in 1964. From 1964-1967 Mr. Voorsanger was an associate of Vincent Ponte, the urban planner, in Montreal and from 1968-1978 was a design associate of I.M. Pei and Partners, New York. Mr. Voorsanger formed his own firm, Voorsanger and Mills, in 1978, subsequently re-organized in 1990 as Voorsanger & Associates Architects, P.C. Since its inception, the firm has gained wide recognition for its built projects, which have been published in Europe, Japan and the United States. The firm has received many local, state, and national design awards. Projects range in size from small interiors and the design of furniture to multi-million dollar residential and institutional buildings.

Mr. Voorsanger's work has been exhibited at the Museum of Modern Architecture, Helsinki; the Harvard Graduate School of Design; Columbia University; Rhode Island School of Design; the Architectural Association of London; The Brooklyn Museum; and the Deutsches Architekturmuseum, Frankfurt. He has also taught advanced design studios or lectured at Harvard, Yale, Columbia, Rhode Island School of Design, Pratt Institute and the University of Pennsylvania among others.

Mr. Voorsanger's principal projects include, in chronological order, the New York University Midtown Center, Le Cygne Restaurant, the Graduate and Undergraduate dormitories for New York University, the International Competition for The Brooklyn Museum Master Plan, The Pierpont Morgan Library, Hostos Community College, New York; the residences of Mr. & Mrs. Leon Hirsch, Mr. & Mrs. Richard Mellon, Ligonier, Pennsylvania; a new sanctuary for the Riverdale Jewish Center, New York; the monorail stations at Jamaica and La Guardia for the Port Authority of New York and New Jersey and the Wethersfield Carriage Museum, Amenia, New York.

▌ Hardware and Software:

Hardware: Macintosh G3
Software: Form•Z and Photoshop

Asia Society, New York, New York

▌ Design Concept:

Asia Society is a ten story building designed by Edward Larabee Bames in the early 1980's now requiring complete transformation of administrative space to public uses such as galleries, museum functions, major garden court, cafe and store. The image shows a major intervention of an existing building ground floor transforming the entry to provide a digital display of the Society's international programs projected onto the transparency of stair and vertical enclosures.

▌ Credits:

Bartholomew Voorsanger, James MacDonald and Aaron Neubert

Wendy Evans Joseph Architect P.C.

E-mail: wjoseph@rosecliff.com

New York, New York 10019

The Rockefeller University Pedestrian Bridge and South Plaza, New York

Profile:

Wendy Evans Joseph Architect PC is a planning, architectural and interior design office established in 1993. As a small practice, the office is unique in that it explores spacial and material ideas at a wide range of scales and program types. The firm is interested in projects that have an impact on our environment; where the client is not just the first hand user but a larger public or entity as well. Wendy Evans Joseph's design is generated from the conditions of the site and the relationships between programmatic elements, not from any stylistic preconceptions. "...Ultimately, our work depends on a quality collaboration witha sensitive owner; with such we are able to deliver a singular design."

After receiving her Master in Architecture from Harvard, Ms. Joseph was with the firm of Pei Cobb Freed & Partners for a dozen years. She is also a winner of the prestigious Rome Prize in Architecture from the American Academy. Aside from her practice, Ms. Joseph is a frequent juror for professional design awards and at various schools. She is the Vice President of the Achitectural League of New York.

Use of Digital Media:

".... All of our firm's work is done on the computer. Our Macintosh network is linked by eathernet to a server and all work is saved on CD's. When we coordinate with associated architects in other cities we use e-mail to send drawings back and forth. This is an effective way to work out of town."

The Rockefeller University Pedestrian Bridge and South Plaza, New York

▍Hardware:

Power Macintosh G3/266, 7300/180, U-Max scanner, Epson Printer, and HP 7000 plotter

▍Software:

Form•Z Renderzone, Adobe Photoshop, MiniCad

▍Drawing Process/Digital Technique:

The plan of the bridge and it's elevation were drawn in Auto CAD14 by the engineers and modified in-house in MiniCad. The Form•Z model was built and then collaged into the photograph of the existing site conditions using Photoshop. Mini Cad drawings served as the first base for developing the three-dimensional model in Form•Z.

▍Concept:

Bridge: The photomontage shows a cantilevered, 180'-cable-stayed bridge over 63rd Street between York Avenue and the FDR Drive in New York City. The pedestrian bridge provides a direct connection from a high-rise housing complex to the laboratory area of The Rockefeller University's campus. In order to avoid extensive renovation of the tower, we span the street with a cantilevered, cable-stayed structure. The cantilevered portion is approximately 140-feet long. The form is uniquely conceived to support the Y-shaped bridge path.

Canopies: Glass canopies and screen walls are part of a stainless steel structure on the plaza. The glass is tinted using a color interlayer between sheets of laminated glass. At the edge, the clear glass overlaps for 2" for a clean silhouette against the sky. All of the steel work and details are coordinated with the bridge, its railings and structure.

Ken Yeang of T. R. Hamzah & Yeang

Malaysia

The Nagoya Expo 2005 Tower, Nagoya, Japan
Business Advancement Technology Centre Mukim of Setapak, Kuala Lumpur
Vertical Park for the URA Singapore Competition Entry 1998

Profile:

The firm T. R. Hamzah & Yeang Sdn. Bhd. was set up in 1976 with the two partners, Tengku Robert Hamzah and Dr. Ken Yeang. Both are graduates of the AA School in London. Tengku Robert completed the AA School's Tropical Design Course under Dr. Otto Koenigsberger. Dr. Ken Yeang received his PhD on ecological design from Cambridge University in Britain. The firm is best kown for their work on the ecological design of large buildings, particularly skyscrapers.

Hamzah & Yeang's Use of Digital Media:

Horizontal texture-mapping (of events, traffic, pedestrian, vegetation, etc.) on to the site in 3D modeling aids in the decision-making for the designers. Vertical texture-mapping studies further extrudes the design in the Y-axis.

Hardware and Software:

Hardware: Power Macintosh, Pentium II, Silicon Graphics 02

Software: Form•Z, Adobe Photoshop, Adobe Illustrator, Softimage, Video Fusion, 3D Studio Max, AutoCAD R14

Drawing Process/Digital Technique:

With the aid of softwares such as Form-Z and 3-D Studio Max, the following are achieved:
-Hybrid photomontage of physical models with 3D-images continue to inform the design during the conceptual design stage.
-Space simulation is utilised via 'Softimage' animation to further explore the event context, urban context and interior spaces. Video playback of the animation provides the Client with an opportunity to visualise space, which can be utilized for marketing purposes.
-AutoCAD R14 is used primarily for production drawings

Design Concept:

The Nagoya Expo 2005 Tower, Nagoya, Japan: The Nagoya Expo 2005 Tower is the alternative proposal as the vertical option to the conventional horizontal layouts used in the previous Expos elsewhere in the world. The vertical solution proposed here addresses the issue of the ecological sensitivity of the site by creating "artificial land" in the sky. In going vertical, the proposal will preserve more than two-thirds of the existing ecosystem of the locality. The tower will be 600m high and will have 50 segments of platforms @ 12m height that will enable the various pavillions to be built (up to 3 stories) within each segment.

The key circulation system is by means of a spiraling monorail with its twin tracks placed on the periphery of the tower with "stations" at 6 segment intervals (i.e. 2 minutes travelling time between stations). This connects to the LRT system at the ground-plane. In addition to these, there will be supplementary systems of elevators, escalators and inclined travelators. However as with most Expos, there will be a main Promenade for use by pedestrians from which all pavillions will be accessible. This Promenade in the tower will be in the form of a large gentle ramp that traverses from the ground-plane all the way up to the top of the tower.

After the Expo, the 50 segments in the tower become real estate assets as "artificial land" in the sky. The tower can be developed with its infrastructure already in place for residential light industrial, commercial and administrative uses.

Credits:

Project Team:
Kiyonori Kikutake (Project Leader),
Shizuo Harada, Ken Yeang,
Tengku Robert Hamzah
Digital Drawing: Ridzwa Fathan.

The Nagoya Expo 2005 Tower, Nagoya, Japan

Business Advancement Technology Centre
Mukim of Setapak, Kuala Lumpur

▌Concept:

The scheme consists of a 47 acres landscaped park within which the buildings are set and is serviced by a central series of public plazas, boulevard walkways and car access routes. The LRT System is integrated into the site with a centralized station at the junction between the retail, commercial and university facilities. The buildings bring together the principles of the bioclimatic approach to the design of tall buildings and urban design developed over the previous decade by the firm.

In particular, the scheme has the following features:
• Landscaping is applied to the entire development. The building is accessed via the landscaped ground plane of the site. Water gardens and soft landscaping enhance the pedestrian routes throughout the site.
• Landscaped and terraced skycourts have been incorporated at the floors of the office towers providing building occupants the opportunity to relax in pleasant surroundings. To maintain connectivity between floors, these skycourts form a continous vertical link, both visually and physically threading together all stories.
• Integrated Building Management Systems control building internal conditions by monitoring the immediate (external) surroundings through a series of environmental sensors located on the roof.

▌Credits:

Principle-in-charge: Dr Ken Yeang
Project Architect: Tim Mellor
Design Architect: Ridzwa Fathan, Chuck Yeoh Thiam Yew, Sam Jacoby, Ravin Ponniah, James Douglas Gerwin
Digital Drawing: Ridzwa Fathan.

Master Plan

Sectional Studies

Business Advancement Technology Centre, Mukim of Setapak, Kuala Lumpur

Vertical Park for the URA Singapore Competition Entry 1998

▌ Concept:

Continuous vertical park as a prototype ecological tower. This 25-storey tower is designed on a 838 sq. meter site situated in the junction of Waterloo Street and Middle Road in Singapore.

▌ Credits:

Principal-in-charge: Dr Ken Yeang
Project Architect: Andy Chong
Design Architect: Ridzwa Fathan
Design Team: Claudia Ritsch, Stephanie Lee, See Ee Ling
Digital Drawing: Ridzwa Fathan.

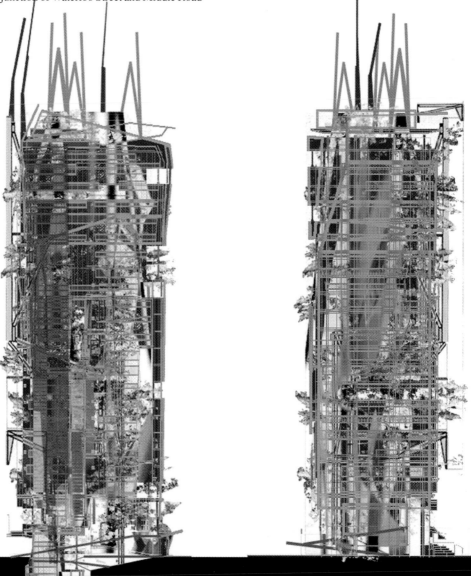

Vertical Park for the URA Singapore Competition Entry 1998

Office Building, Tokyo, Japan, by Kajima Corporation, Japan